Breakthrough Thinking
for
Nonprofit Organizations

Bernard Ross
Clare Segal

Breakthrough Thinking for Nonprofit Organizations

Creative Strategies for Extraordinary Results

THE MANAGEMENT CENTRE

JOSSEY-BASS
A Wiley Imprint
www.josseybass.com

Published by Jossey-Bass
A Wiley Imprint
989 Market Street, San Francisco, CA 94103-1741   www.josseybass.com

Jossey-Bass books and products are available through most bookstores. To contact Jossey-Bass
directly call our Customer Care Department within the U.S. at 800-956-7739, outside the U.S. at
317-572-3986 or fax 317-572-4002.

Jossey-Bass also publishes its books in a variety of electronic formats. Some content that appears in
print may not be available in electronic books.

Jacket illustration © Leon Zernitsky/Stock Illustration Source

Library of Congress Cataloging-in-Publication Data
Ross, Bernard, date.
  Breakthrough thinking for nonprofit organizations: creative strategies for extraordinary
results/Bernard Ross and Clare Segal.
    p.   cm.—(The Jossey-Bass nonprofit and public management series)
Includes bibliographical references and index.
  ISBN 0-7879-5569-8 (alk. paper)
  1. Nonprofit organizations—Management. I. Segal, Clare, date. II. Title. III. Series.
HD62.6 R678 2002
658′.048—dc21

                                                                          2002011290

Printed in the United States of America

FIRST EDITION
HB Printing   10 9 8 7 6 5 4 3 2 1

The Jossey-Bass

Nonprofit and Public Management Series

Contents

Tables, Figures, and Exhibits

To Judy Segal, who practiced breakthrough thinking before we knew what it was, and whose life and work were an inspiration

And to Eileen Ross, who paved the path to allow others to make their own breakthroughs

Preface

We sat down to write this book after spending a number of years working as management consultants with nonprofit organizations in various stages of major change. We had some questions we needed to answer. Why was it that some of these organizations set out with such promise and yet failed to make the breakthrough? How come others that seemed to start in a muddle achieved a radically higher level of performance? What was it that caused some to stall and others to steam ahead?

To try to answer these questions, we decided to review our own work and to look at what others were doing. We looked and we learned and we were amazed, inspired—and sometimes just puzzled—by what we discovered. And we wanted to share what we'd found with as many other people in as many organizations as possible. Before we got around to actually writing a *book*, though, we needed to be sure of our *purpose*. So, being dull management consultants, we came up with a mission: "to inspire managers and board members in nongovernmental organizations (NGOs) to believe they can achieve extraordinary results, and to give them *practical* strategies and techniques for achieving such results." Please judge what follows against that ambitious mission.

If you want to be inspired, you can read about the first Ethiopian direct mail letter, or the Boston hospital that won a prestigious Restaurant Association award for its gourmet-standard food.

We use the word *nonprofit* throughout this book. This encompasses the more general *non-governmental organization* (NGO) and *not-for-profit*.

If you want something quirkier, try Greenpeace's "celebrate failure" awards or the radical alternative job titles of the Council on Foundations.

But inspiration is not enough. Because we're management consultants, our starting point is always this: Does it work in practice? Theories are good for underpinning what we do or explaining why things turn out as they do, but they can be more elegant in the hypothesis than the application. So how does what we've set out to do work in the real world? Who's going to benefit from this book? Here are some examples.

You know what you want to do and how to get there, but you can't seem to bring your staff or board with you. Look at Chapter Ten, which explores people's different responses to change and how you can deal with it most effectively to bring the majority on board. You might also find Chapter Nine useful, as it focuses on challenging the mind-sets that prevent nonprofits from imagining radical change in the first place.

You seem to be stuck on a performance roller-coaster: it improves, it falls back, it improves, it falls back. You just can't seem to break through an invisible ceiling. Look at Chapter Two, on second wave thinking—breaking out of comfort zones and moving up to a radically higher level of performance. Try Chapter Three, on setting breakthrough goals. So-called stretch goals just don't take you far enough anymore.

You're not short on ideas, but you're weak on implementation. Chapter Eight looks initially at balancing creativity and innovation and goes on to explore how to create an innovative culture. Chapter Seven shows you how to organize your thinking to be able to think differently.

There are so many different processes involved in going for breakthrough that you're not sure where you should focus your own energies and where you should get other people to focus. Look at Chapter Ten. There's an entire section on the different roles needed to drive through change and who might be best suited to take them on.

You know you need to change, but you just can't seem to find the springboard idea. Try Chapter Four, which introduces the notion of systematic creativity; then move on to Chapter Five, on releasing creativity.

As you'll see, we've designed the book as a toolbox. Some of you will want to use all the tools, others will have specialist needs. For this reason, the chapters both stand alone and interconnect to allow for maximum flexibility. Please work with what suits you.

We regard this book as work in progress, and we hope you will too. Change is constant. Breakthrough change for nonprofits is *essential* if they are really to make a difference. We've given you a sampler of good practice from around the world; there are also some examples of approaches that haven't worked but that provide valuable learning. Now it's up to you.

August 2002   Bernard Ross
Clare Segal
London, England

Acknowledgments

Thanks to Dorothy Hearst, our editor, whose encouragement and optimism never wavered in the face of missed deadlines and impenetrable British colloquialisms.

Thanks also to the many friends and colleagues who have helped and inspired us, and to the many individuals and organizations who generously helped with examples for the book. A special thanks to George Smith and Ken Burnett. We've always admired their work and approach to work. Read anything by them that you can get hold of.

Heartfelt thanks to all our staff and colleagues at The Management Centre who have put up with our absence of mind, if not body, during the long months of writing this book. Not to mention their keyboarding, critiquing, and—occasionally—praising.

Finally, thanks to our final copyeditor, Michele Jones, who pushed us hard but purposefully at the end.

B.R. and C.S.

The Authors

BERNARD ROSS is codirector of The Management Centre. He is a graduate of Edinburgh University, Scotland, where he studied English. After graduation he worked in community settings using arts and culture as a way to tackle social issues. He was responsible for the first-ever breakfast TV show to be transmitted in the United Kingdom. This was broadcast on a cable network to residents of a large housing estate in the north of England as part of a government-licensed community television experiment. He also won Gulbenkian Foundation and Arts Council awards for further study into the role of video in community action.

Among Ross's publications are *Dunstan Community Television: How We Did It* and *Social Auditing: How to Carry Out Social Audits*.

Since setting up The Management Centre with Clare Segal in 1988, Ross has carried out consultancy and training assignments for many international NGOs including Amnesty International, Greenpeace, UNHCR, Save the Children, and Oxfam. He has worked in countries as diverse as Argentina, the Dominican Republic, Sweden, and Ethiopia. He was involved in designing the first-ever direct mail campaign in Ethiopia, which produced an unprecedented 40 percent response rate. He has also written and spoken widely on strategy and creativity in organizations.

CLARE SEGAL is codirector of The Management Centre, a U.K.-based international management consultancy. She is a graduate of York University, England, where she studied history. After graduating she worked in the field of welfare rights for some time and then joined Community Service Volunteers, one of the United Kingdom's largest NGOs, to run a community history project.

In 1984 Segal set up her own media production company, Connexions. The company produced training videos and publications for the NGO market. Segal won several awards for her work, including the prestigious Best Video Award in the United Kingdom's *Good Video Guide* for her educational video on sexism, *Girls Talk*. This video was a worldwide best-seller and was even bought and smuggled into the Islamic republic of Iran by a liberal NGO. Her other video work covers issues from women's employment in nontraditional jobs to volunteering.

Among Segal's other publications are *The Essential Community Video Handbook*, *Women Work*, *The Guide to Volunteer Organizing*, and *Arts and Unemployment* (editor).

Since setting up The Management Centre with Bernard Ross in 1988, Segal has carried out consultancy and training assignments with some of the world's largest NGOs, including UNICEF, WHO, and HelpAge International. She has worked in countries as far apart as Pakistan, Thailand, Malaysia, and Mexico. Segal specializes in communications and marketing consultancy. She has coached a number of CEOs and senior teams on sharing their vision.

The Change Environment

Why Good Isn't Good Enough Anymore

This book is for managers and board members in nonprofit organizations. It's designed to provide an ideas toolbox for those individuals who want to achieve significant—maybe even breakthrough—change in their organizations, whether that change is in fundraising, service delivery, or all-around performance. We use the toolbox metaphor because we've written the book specifically so you can pick and choose the tools or techniques that work best for you. Bear in mind, though, that some tools are a great deal easier to learn to use than others. Remember too that a toolbox isn't a set of instructions—you still need to have a plan!

The book has mostly arisen out of our consulting and training work with nongovernmental organizations (NGOs) and nonprofits worldwide, especially in Europe, the United States, South America, and Africa. Our company, =MC, is an international consultancy and management training organization. We work exclusively with nonprofit organizations, and our customers include many of the world's largest and most challenging nonprofits, including UNAIDS, UNHCR, Greenpeace International, Amnesty International, and the International Federation of the Red Cross and Red Crescent. We've also carried out assignments for organizations as diverse as the President's Office in Egypt, the Tate Gallery in London, the UK Labour Party, and the Council on Foundations in the United States.

In this book, we aim to provide enough exercises and examples of both disasters and best practice for you to assess how you might avoid the mistakes of others and apply their successes in your organization. Most examples are from nonprofits. Some, though, are drawn from the private sector because they show best practice in our view. The key thing is to be open to learning from whatever quarter it comes.

What we're *not* trying to do is provide a step-by-step, how-to guide to achieving breakthrough. Methods and approaches will differ depending on who you are, on the type of organization you run, and how far you are (or are not) into the process. There is no one way to do it, and the nature of transformations is that they are messy and hard to predict or even manage. Many such efforts inevitably fail in absolute terms. But even in that effort there is great learning. (We'd love to hear more from you; please send examples of your successes and, yes, failures. You can contact us at www.management-centre.co.uk.)

Not Good Enough

This book is a response to a simple but challenging idea that we keep bumping into all the time: *good*, in performance terms, isn't good enough anymore for nonprofits.

In our view, there are three broad concerns that all nonprofits have to face. First, the environment in which you work is changing incredibly rapidly, and you have to "catch up" with this environment just as businesses have had to in theirs. This change process is not just continuous but accelerating. It demands a response if nonprofits are to meet their own ethical guidelines and use donor money efficiently and effectively.

Second, the needs and concerns of those you are striving to help are increasing. At the more brutal end of the spectrum, greater numbers of people in the world are suffering more, and nonprofits involved in the relief of suffering have a moral and business responsibility to respond to the needs of those people. Not all nonprofits are working at the sharp end, of course. Arts and cultural organizations rarely make that claim. But they too can make a significant impact on people's lives, and they too face real challenges: to engage people who feel excluded from arts and culture, to promote user loyalty, and to strive for improvement in performance. Somewhere in the middle, service organizations have to face the fact that they need to meet more—and more sophisticated—demands from their users.

Third, there is increasing competition for resources. Nonprofits seek funds from corporations and individual donors. But so do sports clubs, political parties, universities, schools, and even—in some countries—essential services, such as the police and fire department.

Our perception is that against the background of these three broad concerns, nonprofits increasingly feel that they have to break through to a whole new level of performance. They have to be transformationally better than they are now.[1] Some transformations will come from the sheer scale of the challenge, such as the mass migration of refugees during the Rwandan genocide. Others will be the result of a more prosaic but nevertheless demanding impulse, such as rising costs.

Drivers for Change

If we look more closely at why organizations decide to change, we find the reasons can be divided into internal and external drivers.

Internal Drivers for Change

The following are some *internal* drivers. Which of them applies to you?

- *New mission or vision*. The organization may need a new vision or mission, or it will run out of steam. Recently a major European nonprofit for the blind made a radical change in its organization and business purpose from providing guide dogs to supplying a whole range of new services to people with sight impairment. The change of direction wasn't because the organization could no longer raise money. They were still extremely successful. Their challenge was that almost everyone who needed and wanted a seeing eye dog had been accommodated, yet the organization recognized that sight-impaired people had other needs. The original mission had lost its urgency: they had to change or ossify.

• *The speed of business.* Every kind of organization is having to speed up its processes. Foundations have to process grants more quickly. Relief agencies have to reach refugees more quickly, and certainly before CNN! Our experience of talking to managers at nonprofits suggests that they have had to make more decisions in the last five years than they did previously. And, more challenging, most managers said they had had to make those decisions in less time. Faster is the deal.

• *Cost reduction.* For many organizations the need to reduce costs is a key driver for breakthrough change. During the dot-com boom, for example, many nonprofits in Silicon Valley had to move out of the geographical areas they were set up to serve because of the high cost of office space. They couldn't change the reality of rising property prices, so they needed to focus on new ways to deliver services from a distance.

For health organizations, prevention *has* to work as a way of driving down the cost of treating HIV. A condom costs $.25, but a cocktail of retroviral drugs can cost up to $6,000 *per month*. (Developing countries can't begin to pay these prices, which is why South Africa's legal challenge for the right to manufacture generic drugs was so important. And the success of this campaign—headed by a nonprofit—has proved to be a significant breakthrough.)

• *Service failure.* A number of nonprofits are failing in their purpose, some only a little, some catastrophically. We're sure you can think of at least one nonprofit that's not doing as well as it should. But what about those that fail really badly? At times, the UN is seen by many to fall into this category, especially after the debacles in Sierra Leone and Bosnia-Herzegovina. Another high-profile example is the failure of the Canadian Red Cross to provide a safe blood supply in the 1990s. Because of contamination, many people were infected with HIV. As a result, the Canadian Red Cross had to critically reexamine their practices and structure (and to clear out top management). It was vital that they changed—and were seen to change—to win back public confidence.

> **Most health charities in Africa will be put out of business by water engineers.**

• *New technology.* The opportunities offered by new technology to improve the way nonprofits do business are significant. And, as do commercial organizations, nonprofits strive to take advantage of them. For instance, Nordic Greenpeace has managed to persuade almost 50 percent of its members to receive information and appeals online. The result is that the organization is able to e-mail pictures and news about fast-breaking campaigns as they happen. *And* get rapid responses to appeals. *And* save on postage and printing costs.

New(?) Technology Makes Nonprofits Redundant

It's not just new technology that can help solve challenges. Sometimes old technology works better than new. For example, there are several nonprofits that exist to provide treatment for eye disease in developing countries. Orbis International, with its flying eye hospital, is one. Sightsavers International, with its locally based projects, is another. These nonprofits pride themselves on using the latest and most sophisticated drugs and techniques and bringing them to the poorest people in the world for free.

Both organizations recognize, however, that most eye disease, especially in Africa, is water-borne by parasites. If prevention is the cure, the real cure for most eye disease is clean water, not medication or sophisticated surgery.

This reality led a senior manager of Sightsavers to tell us at a conference, "One day we'll be put out of business by water engineers."

External Drivers of Change

There are also *external* drivers for breakthrough change.

• *A change in public perception.* Some causes suffer from being "hot" and then dropping from people's consciousness. For instance,

HIV and AIDS was a very high profile cause in the United States and Europe in the late 1980s, yet it dropped off the public agenda in the 1990s (this despite the increased level of HIV infection and its significant spread into the heterosexual population). So to create greater awareness of this topic, nonprofits have to look for new tactics to capture public interest and concern.

They also need to think about the public's perception of time. We used to accept that organizations were open to deal with us at certain times. Now much of the expectation is for availability 24/7. To what extent is your organization 24/7?

- *A change in priorities.* Ethiopia was an absolute priority for donor agencies in the developed world in the late 1970s and early 1980s because of the famines. The result was an incredible growth in nonprofits working in Ethiopia: from 150 to 3,000 in the five years from 1978. But as the threat of famine receded, so did the external investment. Nonprofits began to suffer. In the 1990s, when Ethiopian nonprofits found themselves short of money, they began to identify their own country and population as a source of funds. As a result of this thinking, they ran the first telethon in Africa, a massive, eleven-hour show using just one presenter and two cameras. In villages around Ethiopia, people crowded around one TV and had perhaps one phone. The lack of reach was balanced by the fact that villages and neighborhoods often competed to raise money. This rivalry led to significant funds being raised. One environmental nonprofit also sent the first direct mail letters used to raise money in Ethiopia (see below). The money from these initiatives has been used to help create a self-funding welfare structure, less dependent on developed country donors.

Ethiopia's First Direct Mail Letter

Ethiopian nonprofits have begun to look more closely at how to raise funds themselves. For several years, =mc has been running fundraising workshops with an Ethiopian coordinating nonprofit called Christian Relief and Development Agency (CRDA). It brings together nonprofits working in a range of disciplines, such as literacy, water, food security, and environment, and we run a weeklong program.

The focus of most of the program is on raising grants from international foundations and government agencies in the developed world, but for one workshop some three years ago, we agreed to run an extra hour-and-a-half session called "The Future of Fundraising." It covered techniques that we wanted to suggest would eventually arrive in Ethiopia, such as credit card donations, lotteries, and the like. As each technique was briefly discussed it was greeted with polite, if unconvinced, interest. The most skepticism was reserved for fundraising through direct mail letters. "It'll never work—it wouldn't fit with Ethiopian culture," was the view of most of the forty delegates. But one young woman, Nadia Weber, working for an Ethiopian branch of a Canadian-based environmental nonprofit, CPAR, was excited by the idea.

After some discussion with her board, she wrote Ethiopia's first direct mail letter and planned the appeal with colleagues. They hand-delivered the letters to businesspeople, local embassies, and wealthy individuals living in the capital, Addis Ababa—the only place for which they had addresses. The mailing list was just five hundred people, carefully culled from a range of sources. One side of the letter was printed in Amharic, the other in English.

A year later we went back to run another workshop. The young coordinator of the project came along. She explained, rather sadly, that the board was unhappy. She'd had a disappointing response to the letter. Why disappointing, we asked. "Only 40 percent of the people sent back money," was her answer. Forty percent! We were astonished. "Didn't we explain that a normal response is only 2 to 5 percent?" Clearly not. She had written the letter *assuming* a 100 percent response. Sometimes we create too many self-limiting beliefs.

For us a key learning from Nadia's experience was that we too were guilty of assuming—and accepting—that only five or so people in one hundred would respond to a direct mail appeal.

- *Competition for funds and resources.* There has always been competition between nonprofits. The rapid increase in their number means there are more organizations chasing the same sources of money, whether it's from funding partners or, in the case of aid agencies, in the form of contracts from commissioning governments. Indeed, competition for contracts has broadened as the distinctions between nonprofits, the public sector, and the private sector have blurred. For example, private Russian companies now bid against Western nonprofits for aid delivery contracts. Their argument is that it doesn't matter how the aid is delivered, simply that it is delivered quickly and effectively. They have teams of ex-soldiers (with their ex-military equipment) who are less costly and better prepared to take even bigger risks than nonprofit staff. Nonprofits need to deal with this phenomenon; otherwise, paying donors will have difficulty justifying working with them, rather than the equally efficient ex-soldiers, simply because they are nonprofits.

- *A change in technology.* London Lighthouse was a flagship HIV-AIDS project in London, England. It was built as a hospice, providing a wide range of therapeutic services to people who were very ill and dying from the disease. Converted at a cost of $15 million, it quickly fell into disuse as improvements in the effectiveness of combination drug therapy meant that mortality rates plummeted. The technology change made this project as redundant as the Pony Express was after the coast-to-coast telegraph link was completed in the United States.

Which Change Drivers Are Affecting You?

You can make a chart like the one shown in Table I.1 to do a quick audit to see which of these issues have an impact on your organization and to what extent. You can also add issues we haven't touched on. Using a scale of 1 to 10, score each change driver in terms of how important it is to your organization. Add up the numbers for your total score.

Table I.1   Audit of Change Drivers

Issue That We Need to Address	Score (1 = very minor; 10 = very significant)
Internal	
New mission or vision	_____
Speed of business	_____
Cost reduction	_____
Service failure	_____
New technology	_____
External	
Change in public perception	_____
Change in priorities	_____
Competition for funds and resources	_____
Change in technology	_____
Total score	_____

Here's how you can think about your score:

Less than 10: you're working in a stable environment—or you're missing the iceberg that's lurking just ahead.

Between 10 and 50: you're aware of challenges. What are the key ones?

Over 50: read the rest of this book, quick!

The rapidly changing environment—both internal and external—requires that nonprofits change rapidly. And not just change: they have to perform phenomenally better. Much of our work as consultants is with organizations that have made, or are making, that move to transform their performance. This book looks at what they've done and how we've tried to help them.

Summary

Nonprofits, charities, and public bodies are faced with a number of significant challenges that affect the level of performance they need to deliver. Not all of these challenges apply to every nonprofit, but there are three that *do:*

1. The accelerating rate of change in the sector
2. The demand for new services in response to changing needs among users
3. The competition for resources among nonprofits and among nonprofits and public or even private bodies

These three challenges are the key overall drivers for improved performance. They may also, unfortunately, be the factors that highlight the failure of your organization to achieve its potential.

Action

- Conduct an audit in your organization: How future-focused are you in terms of dealing with the key issues you face?
- Identify which of the specific drivers we've discussed are likely to have a major impact, which a medium impact, and which a relatively low impact.

Note

1. You'll find we use the words *breakthrough* and *transformation* interchangeably throughout the book. Between them, we feel, they convey the idea of something groundbreaking, something *radically* different, the striving for which is what this book is all about.

Chapter One

Where Are You Starting Your Breakthrough From?

Strategic Decisions—Simple Choices

The idea of *strategy* sounds very grand, but at its heart, strategy is simple. It involves answering two fundamental[1] questions regarding your organization:

1. Do we know *where* we want to go?
2. Do we know *how* to get there?

The four-quadrant matrix illustrated in Figure 1.1 shows the possible combinations of answers to these two questions. Each quadrant represents a different starting point from which to go for breakthrough. Each quadrant also has positive and negative possibilities.

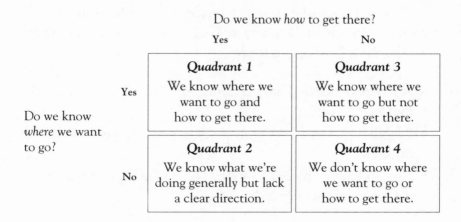

Figure 1.1   Situational Matrix

Quadrant 1: you're clear on where you want to go and how to get there. This can be a powerful position to be in. Your organization has a real strategic focus and powerful techniques to achieve results. However, placing yourself in this quadrant could be an indication of severe self-delusion or unwarranted self-satisfaction.

Quadrant 2: you're confident in your abilities and processes but lack a clear purpose and focus. An organization in quadrant 2 can simply cruise along reasonably successfully. But this can also be a demoralizing position to be in because your energies aren't directed—you have no strong sense of why you're doing what you're doing.

Quadrant 3: you're clear on where you want to go but unclear on how to get there. This can be an energizing position and one that encourages you to look for creative solutions. Or it can cause frustration because the organization isn't bridging the gap between desire and action.

Quadrant 4: you don't know where you want to go or how to get there. You're in the most challenging quadrant. The good news is everyone has agreed that things have to change. But spirits are low, and it's difficult to get people energized. There's also a danger that any energy there is could be wasted, taking you in the wrong direction.

Now it's time to decide which quadrant you think your organization is currently in. Begin by making an initial judgment. Then consider the following questions:

- What evidence do I have that my organization is in the quadrant I've chosen?
- Do other people—staff, stakeholders, funders, users—share my view?
- How did we get to this position? Did it take a long time, or is it a recent phenomenon?

These three questions are important, because:

- You need to be sure you've correctly identified the quadrant you're in. Otherwise you may try to apply an inappropriate strategy for change.

- You need to be sure that other stakeholders share your analysis. If they don't, you need to spend time helping the other stakeholders sign on to it.

- The final question on how long it's taken to get where you are will guide you on whether the challenge is deeply embedded in your organization's culture or something more recent that can be overcome quickly.

Defining the Situation Helps Decide the Approach

Eddie Obeng (1994, 1996), a U.K.-based management consultant, originally developed the situational matrix for project management, but we've adapted it and used it very successfully with nonprofits in more complex breakthrough situations.

The quadrants in the matrix have names that give you a clue to the challenges you'll face if you're in that quadrant. Figure 1.2 illustrates these names, which we call strategic metaphors. Let's look at them in more detail.

	Know How	Don't Know How
Know Where	By the Book	Holy Grail Quest
Don't Know Where	Make a Movie	Wandering in the Fog

Figure 1.2   Strategic Metaphor Matrix

By the Book: Know Where and Know How

We call this strategic approach By the Book because the organization has a really clear idea of where it wants to go *and* is confident and competent in the tactics and approaches it should use. Greenpeace is a good international example. They have a very clear and detailed vision of what they want to achieve, and their way of doing it—through "actions," as they call them—is well established and effective.

People who work in a By the Book organization are usually signed up to both the vision and the strategy, and they're aware, at a very deep level, of how to respond to the situations they find themselves in. For the organization in this quadrant to achieve breakthrough performance it may just need to *do more*, to become *more* efficient, *more* effective at what it already does extremely well. Sometimes specific performance increases come about by applying powerful and well-established techniques to a revised and more challenging vision.

If your organization is By the Book and really *outstandingly* good at what it does, it simply needs to get better at doing more of the same. But you also need to be careful that you're not complacent. It could be that the vision or goals are not really challenging enough. Consider these questions:

- Who says we're "outstandingly good" at what we do? After all, it is possible to be utterly mediocre and still work "by the book."
- Have we conducted an external evaluation of our established techniques?
- Does everyone in the organization share our approach and vision?
- Are the approach and vision ever challenged?
- How are we sure our organization is working at the very top level of possible performance?

Make a Movie: Know How but Don't Know Where

We call this quadrant Make a Movie because in the film industry there's a huge pool of very competent people, but if they don't have a good script to perform to, their expertise is dissipated. Talent and ability aren't enough if you are without focus.

Make a Movie is the quadrant for organizations that have very high levels of expertise and skill but need to improve or even reinvent their vision to provide the *focus* needed to achieve a breakthrough result. Often organizations will be in this quadrant because they've previously set themselves an outstanding goal and achieved it already. The challenge is to find the new goal—and to get excited and energized about it.

UNICEF Christmas card fundraising was in the Make a Movie quadrant for many years. The organization used the card sales as a major vehicle to fundraise for its programs and was *outstandingly* successful. But seeing UNICEF's success, many nonprofits at a national and international level also began producing cards. Between them they made big inroads into UNICEF's market share. To some extent, the agency was caught unawares. Even though a large proportion of its fundraising energy and talent was wrapped up in the production and marketing of Christmas cards, it couldn't win back the share it had lost.

Clearly there was an absolute necessity for the people in UNICEF's fundraising department to refocus and redirect their energy and their talents—to develop a new "where." In the mid-1990s, under Pierre Bernard LeBas, the dynamic director of fundraising, they began to do just that. After undertaking a major review of how the department raised money, they launched a number of new ideas. Many of these built on the department's core competency: direct appeal to individuals. One of their most famous innovations was the envelope in the airplane seat pocket. Passengers are encouraged to put their spare foreign currency into a special envelope found in the airline seat pocket. They then hand it in to the cabin crew. Originally tried with one or two airlines, this program has now been adopted by the One World Alliance (a group of ten of the world's largest airlines), raising almost $15 million to date. (Of course, like all outstandingly successful breakthroughs, this technique too has been copied by many other nonprofits.)

Make a Movie organizations can *seem* to have run out of steam. They appear to be cruising. If it seems possible that your organization is in this quadrant, you might like to think about the following questions to help you develop a clearer idea of where and how to begin changing.

- Is our organization capable and competent, but real focus and drive are missing? It may be that what's needed is a new vision to electrify people and unlock untapped energy.
- What are our core competencies? What are we really good at, and how can we adapt it?
- Could this competency be used elsewhere?
- Are there any new competencies we need so as to cope with the changing environment?

Holy Grail Quest: Know Where but Don't Know How

Holy Grail Quest is one of the most interesting of the four quadrants. Organizations in this quadrant have a powerful shared vision, but they're not clear about how to achieve it. An outstanding example is the leading U.K.-based child-care agency, the National Society for the Prevention of Cruelty to Children (NSPCC).

In 1997, 110 years after the NSPCC's founding, the people there looked long and hard at their mission and how well they were achieving its purpose and decided that their "best" wasn't good enough. Their mission at that time was to broadly support the interests of children. Their income was $130 million a year. They recognized that to have a real, lasting impact on the lives of children and young people at risk they had to provide a transformationally higher level of service. To do that, they had to dramatically increase their income. After a great deal of debate, they agreed to set two overarching and extraordinary goals:

1. To eliminate child abuse within a generation
2. To raise income from $130 million to $410 million within two years

They were absolutely clear about the need and what had to be done to meet it. They identified five vision programs to drive the service change. But then came the "how." How does an organization utterly transform its performance in a way never done before? How does it raise three times as much money as it has ever raised? The truth was that although the NSPCC had good plans, its leaders weren't really sure, in detail, how to achieve these results when they first announced them.

Let's go back to the story of the Holy Grail. In ancient Britain, King Arthur charged each of his twelve knights to find the Holy Grail. (The Grail, you may remember, was the long-lost cup used at the Last Supper. It was one of the most sought-after relics in antiquity and was rumored to have extraordinary healing properties.) Because no one had ever sought the Grail, Arthur couldn't tell the knights either *what* they were looking for or *how* to find it. He even admitted that many of them would fail or even die in pursuit of the goal. Arthur asked them to go off in ones and twos to search. It was important that all twelve knights worked to achieve the same result, even if they did so in different ways.

Likewise the NSPCC had to invent lots of new practice in both fundraising *and* social care to achieve its result. The organization had to go into the transformation prepared to fail but putting all its energy into succeeding. And it had to try a lot of new techniques at once. The Holy Grail approach is a high-risk one involving experimentation and faith. Like the twelve knights, the people of the NSPCC weren't even sure what success would *exactly* look like. They weren't sure precisely how to change their fundraising and service delivery practice to achieve this Holy Grail. (It was partly for this reason that they called their service program the Vision Programs: they were visionary works in progress to achieve a breakthrough result.)

At the time of this writing, the NSPCC has only partly achieved its goal, but already the services have radically expanded and improved. The NSPCC has attracted a lot of attention—and a lot of criticism. It has tried a whole lot of new techniques and has raised a lot of money but not quite managed to triple its income. What's most important, though, is that the organization has challenged the whole way charities in the U.K. do business and the standards of success they set.

By their nature, quests are high-risk ventures, but they can have extraordinary payoffs. They require a very high capacity to change and adapt—and to fail. (Remember, too, the payoff from the original quest for the Holy Grail. The knights never did find it, and many of them perished in the attempt. But their example did have a positive effect never envisaged in the original quest: it inspired the chivalric code used by knights for generations.)

Here are some questions to help you establish if you're on a quest:

- Is our vision clear, urgent, and challenging?
- Is there real excitement about the possibilities and potential but limited ideas on how to focus energies?
- Do we have a sense that our organization doesn't really know how to do what has to be done?
- Do we know, too, that our current practice, no matter how well we engage in it, won't produce the results we need?

Wandering in the Fog: Don't Know How or Where

Wandering in the Fog is a very challenging situation to be in. The organization in this quadrant is in deep trouble. Energy has run out of existing programs and activities, and worse still, there is no clear approach or strategy to deal with the situation—whether it's to bring the organization back on course or to head in a completely new direction. Often organizations don't know that they're heading for fog until it closes in, and that can seem to happen very quickly. Staff, board members, and volunteers do indeed feel as though they're walking through a thick fog. People ask worried questions: "How did we get into this situation?" "What's the right way to go?" "How bad are things?" It's not appropriate to name names here, but we're sure you know some examples of organizations that are Wandering in the Fog.

One such is a theatre in a U.S. East Coast city. It had, in its time, done outstanding radical new work and had attracted unusual audiences who wouldn't normally go to the theatre. But over time the newness of the programs had faded, and with it the audiences. The artistic staff and board, meanwhile, had clustered around two opposed camps. The first camp had retreated into a "People don't understand our theatre because it's too challenging—we should persevere with our artistic vision" frame of mind. The second camp had retreated into "We need to get popular, and soon—it's about survival. Let's throw everything out and start again." The more the audiences shrank, the more each camp's perspective was confirmed. Neither group's perspective changed, and they were stuck.

Wandering in the Fog organizations need serious and urgent action to turn themselves around. Even getting back into a positive direction can represent a breakthrough. But when people are wandering in the fog they can't simply head off in *any* direction. They need a *method* to get them to clear skies. Many organizations are unclear about whether they should go back to what they've done best or go forward to something new but unknown. The one thing they can't do is stay still. Beware: sometimes it can feel like you're wandering in the fog simply because you've had a bad staff or board meeting. Before you finally decide if this is your quadrant, ask yourself these questions:

- Is it unclear why our organization is dysfunctional and how it became so?

- Is there real confusion and conflict about which way to go?
- Among those who agree which way to go, is there disagreement about how to get there?

If the answer to any of these questions is "yes," then you are indeed wandering in the fog.

Risk Analysis

The decision to go for *breakthrough* change is a strategic one. The attempt involves significant risk. You therefore need to carry out some kind of risk analysis.

Risk analysis can be a very sophisticated tool involving complex data mining or financial calculation, but at its most straightforward you need to answer some simple questions:

What's the worst thing *that could happen if our breakthrough went completely wrong?* Would the whole organization die? Would a significant number of users be badly affected, or just inconvenienced? Would we suffer a huge loss of money or prestige?

How likely is it that the worst thing *would happen?* Sometimes it's very likely to happen, other times less so. You need to work that out. For example, if you plan to launch a new database, there's a reasonable chance that it won't work properly the first time. That's OK if all it means is that some appointments are mislaid. It's not so good if cancer screening results are lost.

What can we do to minimize the risk of that worst thing *happening?* What backups do we have? Do we have a Plan B to cope with any potential problems?

How to Respond in Each of the Quadrants

Clearly, the quadrant an organization is in will determine the kind of approach needed for that organization to achieve a breakthrough. Regardless of which quadrant you're in, however, you need to consider four key issues:

1. *Risks and challenges*. What are the potential difficulties? How can we overcome them? What risk does each carry?

2. *Strategy*. How should we organize ourselves? How should we tackle this situation? Who should decide strategy?

3. *Encouraging people and innovation*. What brand-new and what improved ideas do we need? Who should generate them and how?

4. *Leadership*. Where should leadership come from? What kind of leadership style should be adopted? Who should lead?

Table 1.1 on page 22 addresses how these issues play out for organizations in each of the four quadrants.

Summary

All strategy, no matter how apparently complex, boils down to two questions:

1. Do we know *where* we want to go?
2. Do we know *how* to get there?

Each question has two possible answers, yielding a matrix with four possible strategic positions. Your first task is to decide which quadrant you're currently in. If you aren't in quadrant 1, you need to decide how to get out of the quadrant you're in. If you think you are in quadrant 1, you need to decide how to stay there.

Regardless of which quadrant you're in, you need to consider action in four areas:

1. The *risks and challenges* you face
2. The *strategy* you should adopt
3. The approach to *encouraging people and innovation* needed
4. The *leadership* needed

Table 1.1 How to Formulate an Approach to Moving Out of a Quadrant

	By the Book	Make a Movie	Holy Grail Quest	Wandering in the Fog
Risks and Challenges	• Approach can be too formulaic. • Are people excited by the how and the why? • People may get bored and disengage easily. • You may underachieve in terms of potential results.	• Skilled people can make a bad movie! • Radical new movies may need new skills. • Finding the right script (vision) is not easy.	• Is it a quest or a wild goose chase? • Quests involve lots of false hopes and disappointments—how do you keep up morale? • You can't look everywhere—how do you focus energy?	• Morale is very low—"How did we get into this mess?" • Choose the new direction *carefully*. Think through the options. • Is it *possible* to recover?
Strategy	• Define new goals and vision clearly—set them high! • Use the available talents well. • Actively seek challenge from inside and outside.	• Invest time in finding the *right* script (vision). • Work on selling the vision to ensure good buy-in. • Be honest about the skills needed.	• Spend time signing people up to the quest. • Define the quest as best you can in terms of results. • Be prepared to fail a lot of the time and have tactics for dealing with this.	• Gather people together. • Keep communicating with everyone to keep them on board. • Seek advice and consultation.
Creativity and Innovation	• Watch out for comfort zones. • Encourage talent to try new ideas within the framework. • Keep the challenge level high.	• Give good people their head. • Reinforce the vision. • Don't be afraid to modify the vision to make full use of people's skills.	• Encourage all new approaches—you don't know what will work. • Don't assume that experience is best. • Show confidence in people.	• Choose carefully from the available ideas. • Don't go for quick-fix answers. • Encourage *group* creativity.
Leadership Needed	• Set a demanding challenge at the start. • Model the good practice you expect. • Seek to reward and retain your good people.	• Manage and respect the talents available. • Delegate and be hands off. • Build trust and confidence in the team.	• Provide a solid framework for people to work against. • Coach people in their efforts. • Encourage positive attempts, even when they fail.	• Consensual leadership is vital. • Once a decision is made, stick to it. • Avoid promising any quick fixes.

Action

If you haven't done so already, it is time to consider where you are in terms of the four strategic positions. That analysis should illustrate to you where the focus of your breakthrough needs to be: on the *where* or the *how*. Once you understand where you should focus, you can address the questions about risks and challenges, strategy, encouragement, and leadership that are specific to your position.

Note

1. These are the fundamental questions but not the *only* questions you need to answer. In addition to Do we know *where* we want to go? you can ask, Why are we here? How did we get here? What's the good news about being here? And the bad? What is the breakthrough goal? What is the vision? What is the new level of performance we want to achieve? And to Do we know *how* to get there? you can add these questions: What tactics are needed? What are the specific steps? What are the risks and benefits? Who can we learn from? What experience do we have that can help?

Chapter Two

Second Wave Thinking

Moving Toward Radically Different Performance

If you came out of Chapter One concerned about your lack of clarity on the "Do we know *where* we want to go?" question, then this chapter may help. We'll begin by looking at what we call the need-performance gap. What is it, does your organization have one, and is it getting better or worse? This way of considering your organization's performance and how it has, or could, change has strong links to breakthrough thinking. We'll also look at the idea of organizational life cycles and how they relate to performance. Finally, we'll link the ideas of *potential* and *need-performance gap* using the concept of second wave thinking. Second wave thinking, which we will explain in detail later in this chapter, is a way of setting a radically new and higher level of performance, driven by the real need you calculate is present or by the potential for improving your performance.

How Are We Doing?

Leaders of nonprofits need to think seriously about how well their organization is doing. In many nonprofits there is evidence of a failure to respond *significantly* to the scale of the challenges their clients or users face. There's even some complacency. For instance, some organizations proudly boast:

> Our income has gone up by 7.4 percent, and the national average is only 6 percent.
>
> Our visitor numbers increased from 250,000 to 255,000.

We've reduced our overhead by 2 percent.

We've been recognized as a key best value agency.

Our audience for classical music is almost 3 percent young people—that's twice as much as other orchestras.

We secured a quality mark/EFQM award/Baldrige Award.

Now these are not bad claims. In themselves they're good. But the real question such organizations should be asking is this:

To what extent do the improvements and changes we've made actually match up to what's needed?

One way to answer this question is to draw a simple graph with two curves. The first represents what your organization is achieving and likely to achieve over, say, the next three years based on current performance. The second represents the scale of need your organization is supposed to meet. (You might want to guestimate a couple of these.) The difference between the two curves is your organization's need-performance gap. To get a feel for how you might graph your organization's need-performance gap, let's look at the example of WomRef, a refuge for battered women.

The good news from WomRef's point of view is that the organization is expanding its facilities and can take in ten to twenty extra women over the next two to three years. The organization currently accommodates one hundred women in five centers. WomRef is also getting much better at gathering a truer picture of the *scale* of abuse in its city. Unfortunately, the growth in demand for WomRef's services is likely to be exponential. As more women become aware that the centers exist, more women are taking the risk of leaving their abusive partner and coming to WomRef for a secure place to stay. Thus the relationship between the organization's performance and the need it is trying to address looks something like the one in Figure 2.1.

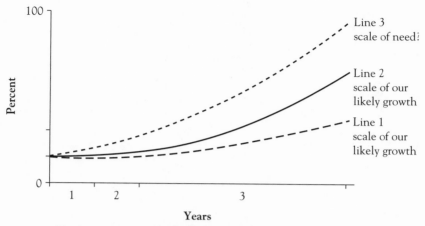

Figure 2.1   WomRef's Need-Performance Chart

WomRef's growth of 10 to 20 percent over three years, represented by line 1, is impressive. However, the scale of need, as shown by line 3, is growing so rapidly that by year 3 it's 70 percent higher than the likely growth of services. Even considering the more optimistic scale of growth (line 2), there is still a gap of 20 percent.

Now it's time for you to graph your organization's need-performance chart. Draw the axes shown in Figure 2.2; label the performance axis to represent any measure that makes sense for your organization. The following are some examples:

- The amount of money you're bringing in through fundraising versus the amount you need
- The number of homeless people you help versus the number of homeless who need help
- The number of young artists you're able to train in your dance company versus the number of young people who would like to train
- The amount of services you can deliver to cancer sufferers versus the number of cancer sufferers

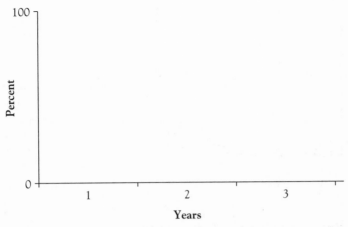

Figure 2.2   Our Organization's Need-Performance Chart

Now draw the two (or three) need and performance curves. Once you've drawn your graph, you can ask yourself these questions:

- Is there a gap between the true level of need we're addressing and our performance in meeting that need?
- How big is the gap?
- Is it growing?

When you drew your organization's chart, did you know how big your need-performance gap is? Or are you so busy with your head down "doing" that it's hard to see the real parameters within which you're working?

Need is one criterion for plotting where you should be aiming to go. But it's not the only possible criterion. You also could work on *potential*—what is possible for you to achieve?

What's the Potential?

Imagine you're the artistic director of a classical orchestra. You plan to play to 90 percent full houses every week. You charge $20. People under twenty-five make up 25 percent of your audience. You have a special rate so that young people can get in for $10—half off the normal price.

You *could* feel good compared to other orchestras, for which only 15 percent of the audience is under twenty-five. Or you could go down to a dance club and see five thousand young people standing in line for up to three hours to pay $30 to hear an "obscure" DJ mixing various tracks in a hot and uncomfortable environment. That might lead you to think of the *potential* audience and the *potential* line outside your concert hall. Then you'd have to think about the extent to which your organization is really meeting the potential need.

List Some Changes

List some changes or improvements that your organization has made to its performance. Alongside that, list the improvement that *could* be made with a bit more effort. In the third column, list the further improvement still needed so as to *meet demand*. The following list shows one example from an organization providing food aid to famine victims.

Improvement Made	Potential Improvement with a Bit More Effort	Improvement Really Needed to Meet Demand
Reduced incidence of food spoilage by 10% by packing it into smaller, discrete cells.	Reduce incidence of spoilage by 30%	Achieve a minimum of 80% unspoiled—preferably 100%; every time inedible food aid arrives, famine victims are brought closer to starvation.

You can use this kind of audit to highlight significant *performance gaps*. Your organization needs to deal with these gaps—they illustrate your potential to achieve.

The Second Wave

Second wave thinking is most easily expressed visually. Every organization has a life cycle of growth, stability, and decline in its performance. This life cycle can happen over many years or just a few years. Second wave thinking involves looking for a point just before an organization's performance seems likely to peak and then taking action to kick performance up to a whole new level. (See Figure 2.3.)

In our experience, the majority of organizations need to *transform* their performance either to have any real impact on the need-performance gap or to achieve their potential. That's where second wave thinking comes in. It's a way of thinking about new—breakthrough—levels of performance that can and must be achieved. It's a way of getting people excited and energized about what might lie *beyond* the current performance horizon. It's a metaphor for potential. It's also a way of linking your performance not to an internal goal but to the needs of the constituency you are striving to serve, giving your organization an external focus. To achieve this external focus, there are some questions you need to answer:

- What is the *real* level of need for our services? How do we know this?

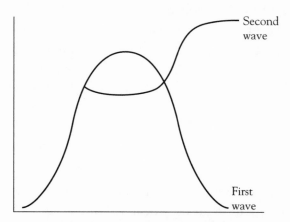

Figure 2.3   Second Wave Thinking

- Can we meet that level? Should we aim for it even if we can't meet it?
- Should we "go it alone," or should other organizations try to meet the need or at least contribute? (See the sections about MBWO and mind-sets in Chapter Nine.)

The starting point for second wave change is a standard and well-established marketing concept, the *life cycle*. Most products, ideas, political parties, fundraising techniques, and the like go through a classic life cycle, represented by a sigmoid curve, as illustrated in Figure 2.4. This curve can, of course, be shorter or longer and of varying amplitude.

We can also apply this very broad concept to the growth of an organization in terms of its performance, as illustrated by Figure 2.5 on page 32.

Although not every organization life cycle looks like the one in the figure, most organizations do begin by being relatively small in impact; they grow to maturity and finally decline. An organization can stay mature over a long or short period of time. Some, such as the International Red Cross, have a very long cycle time so that the period of maturity looks more like a plateau than a curve, as shown

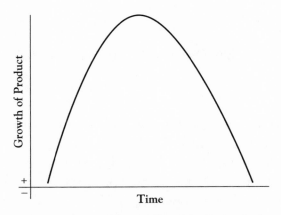

Figure 2.4   Classic Product Life Cycle

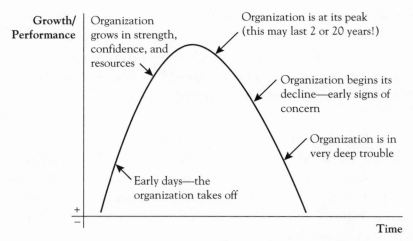

Figure 2.5   Life Cycle of a Typical Organization

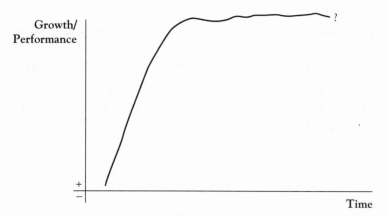

Figure 2.6   Life Cycle of the International Red Cross

in Figure 2.6. In contrast, the life cycle of an exciting, off-beat, experimental dance company might look like Figure 2.7: a burst of raw energy and being "what's hot" followed by an equally sudden falling out of fashion. A campaigning organization might be set up on a tidal wave of popular opinion, only to decay slowly over time (Figure 2.8).

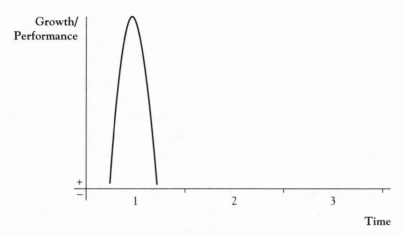

Figure 2.7   Life Cycle of an Experimental Dance Company

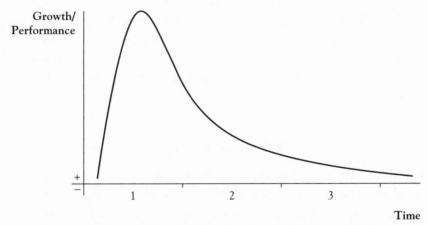

Figure 2.8   Life Cycle of a Campaigning Organization

When looking at and drawing these curves, you need to be clear about what's being assessed. There are different measures of "impact" you might want to consider: income, membership, sales, or even just popularity. Further, it's perfectly possible for your organization to be at its peak membership yet have a declining income. The graphs we've looked at so far need to be considered in the light of this possibility. The one certainty, though, is the inevitability of decay.

Think about your organization. Choose an appropriate scale over time and a measure you feel is appropriate. Easiest to work with are *quantitative* measures, such as money, members, number of people helped, and so on. For a rounded picture of your position, you could draw more than one life cycle and overlay one on the other. So if, for instance, you draw one cycle measuring the amount of money raised and another cycle measuring the number of people helped, you may discover that you're helping fewer people with more money.

The most interesting—and most complex—performance measure to put on the axis is "achieving mission," just because it is so hard to measure. If you want to do this, we would suggest you work with colleagues to come up with four or five key success indicators that you can plot on individual cycles and then overlay. This will give you a broad, general picture of where you are. Remember, though, that the life cycle is a *conceptual* tool, which means you need to live with a degree of ambiguity in the outcome.

Once you've established the measure(s) you want to use and an appropriate time scale, it's time to plot your organization's life cycle to date.

Where to Change?

If your organization is going to try to change and improve, there are good and bad places on the cycle to make the attempt. The main challenge is to decide *where* in the cycle to change. In the second wave model, there only are a few windows of opportunity, or points on the curve, where real breakthroughs can take place. Our experience suggests there are four potential change points. Each has its drawbacks and advantages. The *disadvantages* are illustrated in Figure 2.9.

The advantages of each of these points are listed here:

Point 1. Things are not set in stone, and not too much has been invested. The organization can change here.

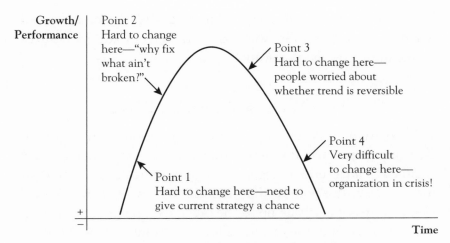

Figure 2.9   Potential Points for Change

Point 2. You're on a roll; there's momentum. Things are good. People are confident and able, and they relish challenges.

Point 3. People accept that there's a need to change. What was working has gone off the boil a bit.

Point 4. It's absolutely certain that things have to change. The current situation is insupportable.

Give some thought to where in the cycle you think it's best for an organization to change, and why. You may want to write down some of your ideas. Also consider your own organization, asking the questions here:

- On the graph of our organization's life cycle to date, are we at position 1, 2, 3, 4, or somewhere in between?
- What evidence do I have that we're at this position?
- Where would my colleagues and other stakeholders place our organization?

Your organization may well have been through this process before. At what points has your organization changed in the past?

Are you in a cycle of only changing in a crisis? Or if you've changed when your organization was experiencing upward or positive momentum, how did that work?

First Waves and Comfort Zones

Our experience suggests that most organizations don't agree to change until just over the crest of their peak, at point 3 in Figure 2.9 (marked by an asterisk in Figure 2.10). One difficulty with attempting change at this point is that "success" *can* end up being defined simply as making it back up to the previous level of performance. This then becomes the first wave level or "comfort zone," as illustrated in Figure 2.10. The comfort zone is a safe area of ups and downs within which the organization may operate for five—or fifty—years. Performance gets better, declines, improves again, but never really *transforms*. The comfort zone thus becomes the organization's operational area.

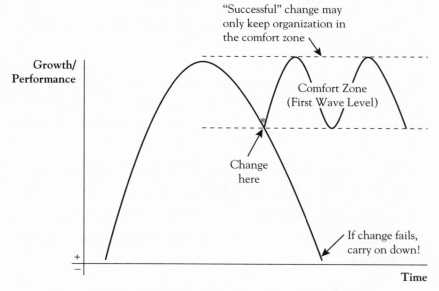

Figure 2.10   The First Wave Level or Comfort Zone

Many organizations stay working in the comfort zone, whether it's in terms of their fundraising, their service standards in customer care, the type of art exhibited, or the time taken to deliver relief supplies. A comfort zone can even receive external validation when similar organizations benchmark themselves against one another in the form of performance rankings of performance. This unconscious collusion sometimes leads to a complacent culture of "safety in numbers-me too" performance: "We're as good as our competitors." So you may not feel you're actually in decline in terms of the cycle. But are you perhaps merely "comfortable"? Is your performance stable, but need is growing exponentially? What is your organization's comfort zone, or the comfort zone in your industry or area of operation?

Where to Change for the Second Wave

Our experience suggests that in the second wave model, the best place to change is *just before the first wave peak*, at point 2 in Figure 2.9. Doing so allows your organization to kick up to a significantly improved level of performance—a second wave. There are good reasons for this:

- You have some momentum already.
- You may well have some political or financial "capital" to drive the change.
- People feel "up" about the organization.
- It's possible to see what peak performance in current terms looks like—the top of the curve—and that it's definable and achievable.
- People can get a real sense of what they can do to reach that level of achievement.

Figure 2.11 on page 38 illustrates the second wave level.

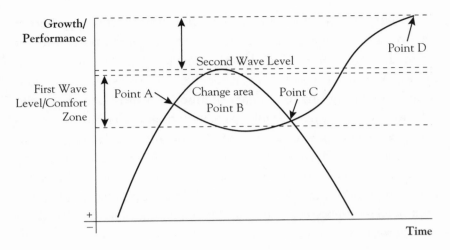

Figure 2.11   The Second Wave Level

Challenges in Choosing a Change Point

Let's imagine, for a moment, that you are in charge of leading a breakthrough initiative. You need to consider the following questions before you decide your action:

- How do you know *when* you've reached point A? Why change here? How do you sell people on the idea of changing? (You'll find useful information on this in Chapters Eight and Nine.)

- What goes on in an organization when in the Change area? How should you behave as a manager or board member? How will staff feel? How do you promote joint learning? What might be the implications for existing service users, customers, funders? How will you maintain momentum when things seem to be going awry? (See Chapters Six and Eleven for help on this.)

- How do you know when you're at point C? How do you sell change to your people when you're here? How do you get stakeholders to rally behind you? (See Chapter Ten for advice on change.)

- How do you *set* point D? What is a *reasonable* level of transformational performance? What competencies, skills, and resources do you need to achieve that level? How can you create a vision of that level that people can relate to? (To find inspiration for how to create the vision, go to Chapter Three.)

- How do you know what activities and actions will help you reach point D? Once you're there, how do you sustain it? What's the role for board members, managers, and even consultants? (To find out more about roles and sustainability, consult Chapters Three, Ten, and Eleven.)

Working in the Change Area

A crucial issue to consider is the question of what goes on in the Change area. Again, based on our experience, things are likely to get worse before they get better. This is perfectly normal. It's a bit like deciding to take formal tennis lessons after years of teaching yourself to play and seemingly playing quite well. You go to meet your coach. She tells you that to improve your game, you have to start by unlearning habits that are actually *preventing* you from achieving a higher level of skill and competence. The result is that you miss the ball—a lot—and normally in front of a class of twelve-year-olds. You then have to rebuild your technique. But it's only when you've gone through the pain barrier of unlearning the old that you can run with the new. And the same is true of organizations beginning the push to the second wave. (To find out more about what to do about learning and unlearning and the roles people play, see Chapters Six, Nine, and Ten.)

Not surprisingly, when organizations are in the Change area there is a major challenge for managers and boards in terms of *their* role. We see them as needing to

- Acknowledge that people will feel uncomfortable during this phase.
- Give people a sense of how long it will take to work through the phase.
- Set some achievable milestones within it.

- Secure the resources to work effectively within this phase and come through.

Worse Before Better

We were working with a major U.S. nonprofit on customer care and customer service. The organization had hired us to help it with a substantial program of consultancy and training on customer care. The nonprofit had spent $50,000. We were making our presentation to the board. Our first overhead transparency contained these words: "Our customer care work should increase the number of complaints over the next 12–18 months by 60 percent."

There was a stunned silence. "Surely," the chair of the board said, "you mean *reduce* by 60 percent?" "Nope," we said, "increase." We then walked them through the logic:

- Most people don't complain because they think you can't or won't fix the service.
- If you install good customer care procedures, people do believe you might fix things.
- Every customer care program we've ever run has resulted in increased complaints *initially*.
- It's a different, but linked, challenge to deal with those complaints.

They got the message.

Nice Idea—How Do You Do It?

Once people are committed to and excited by the *idea* that they might be able to achieve the second wave, fantastic organizational and individual energy—both of which are vital for effective breakthrough—can be unleashed. At some point this energy needs to be channeled and molded into achievable chunks. We look at how to do that in Chapter Three.

For the moment, think about such a change as being a phenomenon comprising both pleasure and pain. This perspective harkens back to a fundamental motivational impulse. Human beings tend to do things for one of two clusters of reasons: we seek to gain the positive payoffs, the advantages, the *pleasure*, and we seek to avoid the disadvantages, the negative consequences, the *pain*. Often, the temptation is to sell the second wave—or any change—on the basis of the positive payoffs: "Think how good things will be if . . .," "We'll be able to feel so proud of what we've done . . .," "We'll have enough resources for . . ." Pleasure is indeed a powerful motivator. People will sign up to the positive payoffs. They will feel attracted to a glowing vision and to possibilities.

But pleasure alone is rarely enough, and you shouldn't forget the power of pain, of people's urge to avoid the negative consequences of not signing up: "Think how much we'll let people down if . . .," "We'll feel so ashamed we didn't achieve . . .," "We won't have enough resources to . . ." The desire to avoid pain can equally be an impetus to move away from a less successful state.

To ensure you avoid comfort-zone thinking, consider using a carrot-and-stick approach to achieve breakthrough results. When constructing your case for change, or for the second wave, there are several key issues to consider:

- How you present your *strategy*
- What *words* you'll use
- What the *movement* will be (toward a positive or away from a negative situation)
- How people will *feel*
- What their fundamental *motivation* will be
- What the impact on *internal others* will be
- What the impact on *external others* will be

Each of these issues can be framed in terms of both pleasure and pain. (Table 2.1 gives you some ideas.) Try to make sure that your breakthrough message addresses most of these issues. Try, too, to ensure that your message contains appropriate pain and pleasure elements for the various stakeholders involved. Doing so will help them sign up to developing organizational momentum. (However you sell the ideas, make sure you sell them to the whole brain and to the whole organization. For information and suggestions on how to communicate the positive impact of making the change and the negative impact of not making the change, see Chapters Five and Seven.)

Selling the Vision

A small theatre company has been left a very generous bequest on the condition that the company use it to build a new theatre. The director of the company sees this as a fantastic opportunity to grow: larger capacity will mean increased revenues, which will allow them to spend more not only on production but also on the fledgling education program. She needs to convince her staff that such an opportunity is too good to miss. She calls them together.

"As you all know, Lileth Jonson has left us $25 million on the condition that we use the money to build a new theatre. I realize that for some of you at least, part of the attraction of being with the company is the fact that we are small. You can swap in and out of different jobs. We know our regular audience by name. And it's true, these things *are* wonderful. Not only that, but force of circumstance has made you all uniquely flexible and multitalented.

"The downside, though, is that despite our continuing capacity audiences, we are lurching from one cash crisis to the next. We simply don't have enough seats to bring in the money we need. Yes, our funders like what we do, but they're concerned that we've reached the peak of our revenues. They feel quite strongly now that they can't keep supporting us at the current level.

"Our audience is loyal? Yes, our audience *is* loyal—but also mostly older. And so, we have a reputation as an older, safer kind of theatre. Meanwhile, what about the younger people in this town— what have they got? Parents want to take their children to the the-

Table 2.1   The Case for Change: Pleasure and Pain

Issue	Pleasure	Pain
Strategy	Powerful positive new vision	Dissatisfaction with status quo
Words	"We can do it."	"We can't *not* do it."
Movement	Toward and up	Away and down
Feeling	Attraction, real joy	Avoidance, real sadness
Motivation	Pride and achievement	Embarrassment and failure
Impact on internal others	Deliver results, align people to action, bring them along	Let people down, see them drift away and become disenchanted
Impact on external others	Deliver better service and benefits to help	Let people down, and see them disappointed

atre. Schools are teaching texts that never come alive for their students because the stories stay on the page. If we don't catch them young, if we don't make the theatre a lively, exciting place for children and young adults to come, we'll lose our audience of the future before they have ever arrived.

"I'm not saying for a minute we need to choose *either* the elderly *or* the young. Because with this new theatre we can cater to *both*—even at the same time sometimes. Come and look at the architect's model. See, we'll have two auditoriums: the main theatre and a studio workshop for experimental productions and school classes. We've been trying for two years now to get the education program off the ground but have repeatedly come up against lack of space. That won't be a problem here. And speaking of space, there's a separate rehearsal room—look, here on the model—which will mean an end to those constant negotiations over whether the next or current production should have priority during the day.

"See, here we've got a café, which will be open from 10 A.M. through to an hour after the end of each performance. The corner we have now from which to sell coffee and cake in the intervals barely breaks even some months, and often runs at a loss. The café alone is projected to bring in $100,000!

"This is *so* exciting. At last we'll have the space to grow, to bring in new audiences while looking after our loyal supporters, and to reach our true potential."

Look carefully at this speech. Notice how in addressing the issues the company director very specifically uses pain and pleasure in various amounts. To sell your new idea you're going to have to consider using similar techniques as a way of helping people sign up to your vision and change.

Summary

Every organization has a life cycle of unique amplitude and length. We can measure our growth or performance in lots of ways: money raised, number of people helped, and the like. There's also an overall measure called "achieving mission." Plotting where your organization is on the cycle can be interesting and challenging.

Organizations decide to change at various points in their life cycle and for different reasons. Each of these key points has advantages and disadvantages. The challenge with the most common change point—just past the peak—is that it leads to comfort-zone work. We want you to break out of comfort zones, and one way to do that is to think about the idea of a second wave: a new, dramatically improved level of performance.

To drive that change you need to create a vision of the new performance level and to create some positive and negative drivers for it: pleasure and the avoidance of pain.

Action

- Draw the life cycle of your organization to date. (Make sure you're clear about what performance or growth you're measuring.)

- Use a graph like that in Figure 2.2 to plot both the *potential* for your organization and the level of *need* that actually exists.

- Explore the *positives*, the pleasurable elements to this second wave level of performance, as well as the *negatives*, the painful elements of not achieving it.

Chapter Three

Setting Breakthrough Goals

Moving Beyond Stretch Goals

In our work helping organizations achieve breakthroughs, we've found it useful to introduce different language to describe new ideas. This language, drawn from a whole range of sources, can help liberate people's minds in terms of how they think they can act. It can help capture a new spirit of organizational culture or a particular type of goal. (*Second wave thinking* is itself an unusual phrase designed to grab people's imagination.)

New Language for New Ideas in Politics

There are a number of examples of different or new language being used to introduce or capture the essence of new ideas. The "New Deal" is a famous U.S. example. Note, as in the examples below, that sometimes the idea works and sometimes not.

• *Joined up government:* coined by the British Prime Minister Tony Blair to describe his new approach to integrated government services and policy. This phrase was successfully used to sell his second-term election in 2001.

• *Glasnost and perestroika:* two words introduced by Mikhail Gorbachev in the 1980s to describe new ways of thinking in his "new" USSR. In retrospect, these words excited more enthusiasm in the West than in the USSR. And Gorbachev, unfortunately, failed to achieve either glasnost or perestroika.

New laungage doesn't need to be about "big" ideas. Every organization has its own internal language. For example, at the annual general meeting a former CEO of the international development agency Traidcraft Exchange (a European fair trade agency) used to hold up signs displaying the organization's annual goals and ask staff to rate their success in terms of "raspberries" or "cheers." Staff had to vocalize their response. (Loud cheers = success; loud raspberries = failure.) Their "votes" were marked on a giant score chart. "Raspberries" and "cheers" became synonyms for success and failure.

Two Distinct Kinds of Change

The words we use carry enormous power. Two words that have proved exceptionally useful for us in setting new kinds of goals are *kaizen* and *horshin*. They are exceptional because they describe not only the *nature of the goals* an organization has to reach but also the *change processes* that it has to go through. We find it useful to use these two words in their original Japanese form rather than in translation. In a way, the "otherness" of the words helps people understand that a change in *thinking* is a precursor to a change in *performance*.

The origin of kaizen and horshin goes back to the end of World War II when Japan, possibly more than any other country involved in the conflict, was at a seemingly catastrophic low point. When they surrendered in August 1945, two of their major cities, Hiroshima and Nagasaki, had been flattened by atomic bombs. The emperor, the "father" of the nation, had admitted his fallibility and given up power. Japan's industrial sector, wired up for a lost war effort, was virtually at a standstill. The people spoke a language used by no one else in the world. They were occupied by a foreign force that had beaten their once invincible army. They didn't have—and still don't have—any natural resources such as oil. It seemed they had little potential to become a powerful force in the world. The choice for Japan at that time was whether to sink—and become an economy largely dependent on outside aid—or swim.

As history shows, Japan chose the second route and in the 1970s, 1980s, and early 1990s became one of the most powerful economies in the world. (At the time of this writing Japan is up against some serious economic challenges, but its current performance doesn't detract from what the country *did* achieve.) Despite all the disadvantages under which it labored, Japan set out on the path to becoming an industrial leader. Out of these desperate times came the parallel philosophies of kaizen and horshin. They began as ways of thinking about industrial performance but have come to be much more widely applied.

Kaizen

Kaizen is a process of slow, continuous, incremental change that leads, over time, to significant improvement in performance (illustrated by Figure 3.1). It's a *constant* search for ways to make *existing* things better, whether you're working with systems, services, or procedures. The journey to change using kaizen is systematic, step-by-step, and "forecastable"—that is, you know where you're going and where you'll end up. The individual changes introduced are small, but they add up to major improvements given enough time.

The Japanese applied kaizen to a whole range of activities, including their car industry. Over twenty-five years, they *transformed* the quality of their cars from the butt of jokes to an international benchmark for safety, style, and reliability. They didn't do this by

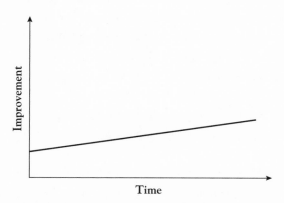

Figure 3.1   Kaizen: Slow, Continuous Improvement

inventing any radical new technologies for cars. They did it by setting a long-term, world-class performance goal and then breaking that goal down into small, achievable chunks. They set out to improve the quality of the rustproofing, then the interiors, then the engines, and so on. Their method was to study what worked elsewhere and to build on existing best practice.

Central to the whole process was a bottom-up philosophy of change: management encouraged and empowered ordinary shop-floor workers to come up with ideas on how to improve things. This approach led to the development of quality circles—a model first promoted in the United States by the quality guru Deming and, ironically, initially rejected by many U.S. manufacturers. From this process emerged a powerful and effective car industry well able to hold its own in the global market.

Quality Circles: What Did You Change Today?

Quality circles are now used worldwide and in many industries, but when they were first introduced they were a revolutionary change. There are two key aspects to them: (1) workers are made responsible for their *own* quality checks, and inspectors are removed; (2) workers are also asked to meet in groups *every day* to discuss what small changes they can make to improve performance or quality.

In a car factory this means that workers have to "sign off" their own work as being of good quality before passing it to the next stage. More important, perhaps, are the daily meetings. Workers have to sit down in a circle at the start of the day and spend twenty minutes answering one question:

What specifically and precisely will you
change and improve today?

The great majority of the time, the changes suggested are very small ones—for example, "I'll try using the wrenches in a different position to see if that makes the process quicker." But these small changes cumulatively make a huge difference.

How many of us working in "empowered," engaged nonprofits find that we sit down even once a week to consider this question? What impact would it make if we were to add up the thousands of small improvements we're currently failing to make?

This process does take place at some charity telephone helplines. Every evening before sitting down to answer calls, helpline workers discuss the previous evening's work to see how they can improve it. This effort might include

- Listening to a recorded call and analyzing what went well or less well

- Seeing how different lighting in the call center room might help improve call handling

- Using different versions of client forms to study how they affect the way data are captured

The kaizen philosophy has since been taken out of a purely Japanese context and applied to a whole range of business and non-business processes. In the not-for-profit world, for example, direct mail fundraising is a kaizen process. There's unlikely to be any revolutionary change an organization can make to radically improve its rate of return on direct mail *in a single pass*. Instead, people test and implement small changes: working with long copy or short, using enclosures or not, producing handwritten or computer-generated letters, sending letters from a patron or a beneficiary, and so on. The increase in income from these small changes might be in the region of 0.2 percent—a tiny amount by itself, but significant in the cumulative results. This process is documented brilliantly by George Smith in his book *Asking Properly* (1996). He shows how tiny changes in direct mail copy, layout, and offer can dramatically improve performance.

At a conference of the U.S. Council on Foundations we attended in Washington, D.C., in 2000, grantmakers reported to us that much of their grant-giving processes are the result of years of careful stewardship and reflection. They build their approach on past experience. They examine the impact their policy has and only change it after careful reflection. Likewise, over the last one hundred years the International Committee of the Red Cross has developed a number of tried, tested, and refined procedures and approaches when mediating in conflict situations. These procedures are carefully documented in their excellent relief and emergency manuals.

The Grameen Bank

The Grameen Bank is an informal banking network in Bangladesh. It was set up almost twenty years ago specifically to enable poor people—and Bangladesh has some of the world's poorest—to have access to credit. Members can use the credit to set up microenterprises or to pay for houses or other necessities. The bank works like a village-based credit union.

At the start the bank was very small, and there was a lot of suspicion and nervousness about it, both from prospective users and from agencies, such as the World Bank, that were asked to provide capital. But gradually it has built itself up, village by village, until it is now the largest bank in Bangladesh—even though it handles only very small amounts of money in each transaction.

This process of slow, incremental growth in performance has been extended to other areas. For example, the bank has now set up its own mobile telephone network. The idea is that the bank provides one person in each village with a mobile phone. That person allows other villagers to use the phone on an as-needed, call-by-call basis. The bank plans to increase the number of phones to seventeen thousand over the course of five years—slowly but surely.

Advantages of Kaizen

There are several advantages to the kaizen approach:

- It involves everyone in the organization: kaizen is a systematic and interactive version of the suggestion box.

- It's a bottom-up process that empowers staff and managers by asking them to take control of improvement.

- Because everyone contributes and sees that his or her contributions are valued, kaizen encourages a high level of buy-in.

- It doesn't put people under pressure to come up with the "big idea"; it's about a series of small improvements having a cumulative effect.

- It's low risk: it doesn't require everyone in the organization to put what he or she is doing on hold and go all out to achieve some great leap forward.

- It has a longish time frame, so there are no urgent deadlines to meet.

- People can come on board slowly; there's plenty of time to bring them around.

These kinds of benefits help to bring many stakeholders on board. They also are helpful in keying into the broadly democratic and inclusive philosophy of many nonprofits.

Disadvantages of Kaizen

Of course, kaizen also has its disadvantages:

- By definition, kaizen takes a long time: if you've got a BIG goal, such as "eradicate homelessness throughout the United States," slow, continuous improvement may take too long. It will certainly be too long for homeless people. They might reasonably ask, "What good is a breakthrough goal if there'll still be another two or three generations of people sleeping on the streets before homelessness is eradicated?" Similarly, if you have a crisis—an earthquake, flood, or other disaster—you're unlikely to have time for the ongoing formal reflection that kaizen requires.

- It relies on *lots* of small ideas to be effective: if kaizen is not handled well as a *process*—if, for example, ideas aren't seen as being welcomed and seriously considered, or if ideas only from certain layers of the organization are taken up—there won't be enough continuous stimulus to bring about change.

- The lack of a demanding deadline may mean that the process runs out of steam. It can be hard to keep people motivated if there's not an end in sight that they can connect to. It may start to be seen as a Sisyphean task that people feel is ultimately hopeless. There's the danger that kaizen becomes an excuse for inaction—even for poor performance.

- The lack of strong direction and focus inherent in kaizen *can* make the process liable to wander off course. If the overwhelming drive isn't there to keep people on track, energies may become misfocused; for example, the nonprofit ends up improving the layout of its aid request form instead of looking at how to create greater access to funds.

- Measurable improvements at any given point may be *very* small, so people need a long-term perspective to appreciate the significance of the change *overall*. This may mean that boards, staff, and managers with long service records are needed to provide the organizational perspective. Newer people may perceive no real change and thus become dispirited.

When planning breakthrough change, it's very tempting to think only of the exponential leap that is horshin (as we will be discussing next). Indeed kaizen *can* seem to work against transformation. However, far from being comfort-zone work, kaizen processes can be used to make focused, incremental improvements in performance toward a breakthrough goal. Kaizen is a useful tool if we have a longish time frame, a clear goal, and a set of processes to gather and quantify knowledge on what works.

Horshin

Whereas kaizen is about steady, continuous improvements, *horshin* is about sudden, exponential, discontinuous, and radical change that leads to dramatically improved performance in a relatively short space of time. Clearly it's not a comfortable process. When using horshin, the exact new performance level is hard to specify. It can go up and then down again, as Figure 3.2 shows.

The initial push in horshin is very different from a kaizen initiative. Usually driven from the top, horshin is based on a strategic impulse: a new technology, a vision, an opportunity, a crisis—or even a hunch.

For an example of horshin, let's look again at Japan. This process was used in the late 1970s by Akio Morita, at that time the chairman of Sony. He was in his sixties, and he loved listening to classical music and liked to have it playing as he worked and relaxed at home. All was fine until his teenage grandson came to stay. His grandson, like many teenagers at the time, was into rock and heavy metal. Morita and his grandson were, apparently, on a collision course.

But Morita didn't want to tell his grandson that he couldn't play his music. Instead he decided to use one of the battery-powered cassette players Sony manufactured. He used his belt to strap the cassette player around his waist, plugged in some earphones, and listened to the music *he* liked without disturbing, or being disturbed by, his grandson.

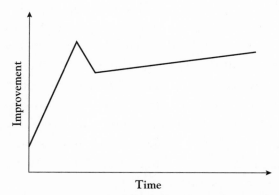

**Figure 3.2   Horshin: Sudden, Exponential, Discontinuous
Change Leading to Radical Improvement**

Morita's improvisation worked to the extent that he could listen to classical music as he moved around the house. But the large cassette player—about the size of two paperback books taped together—wasn't very comfortable to wear. Every time he wanted to sit down he had to take it off, or it would dig into his ribs and thigh. By the end of the day, Morita was thinking, "This is ridiculous. What I need is a cassette player small enough to fit into my pocket." And from that insight emerged the beginning of a horshin change in cassette players: the Sony Walkman.

It was not all clear sailing, however. Morita took his vision to the board. The board was made up of successful businessmen like himself, all in their fifties and sixties. Their first response was skeptical. Would there be any demand for a small personal cassette player you could listen to as you walked around? They suggested that they get a consultant to run some focus groups to see if people would be interested in such an idea. A month later, the consultant came back and said no.

But Morita was the boss, and he had a vision. He told the board to go ahead and get the machine into production anyway. This was done, and just a couple of months later, the first Sony Walkmans appeared in Tokyo's most up-market electrical and department stores. They were priced at the equivalent of $400. They did not sell. Morita ordered the price to be reduced to $300. Still they did not sell. Nor did they sell at $200. At $100 they sold out within days.

So what had happened? The focus groups said they wouldn't be interested, yet there were phenomenal sales at the $100 mark. Why, apparently against all the odds, did the Sony Walkman suddenly take off? There are two reasons. The first is that the success was not actually "against the odds." The focus groups were misprofiled. The profile the board had asked the consultant to test were groups of people much like themselves: middle-aged businesspeople. Of course these groups said no, they wouldn't be interested. As it turned out they simply were not the target market.

The second reason the Walkman suddenly took off at $100 was that at that point it had reached a price that the *actual* market could, with a bit of a struggle, afford. The actual market was young people like Morita's grandson who wanted to be able to take their music with them wherever they went.

The Walkman rapidly became Sony's most successful and profitable product. Certainly at one time the Walkman seemed to be the most widely used personal electronic device on the planet.

Hospital Food Goes for a State Award

Hospital food is rarely praised.[1] Sometimes it seems that the height of hospital caterers' ambitions is to avoid prolonging a patient's stay because of food poisoning.

That standard wasn't nearly high enough for Helen Doherty, director of dietetics for Massachusetts General Hospital (MGH) in Boston. She didn't want just to produce edible food. She set herself the horshin goal to produce excellent food so outstanding that even nonpatients would *choose* to come to MGH cafés and outlets to eat.

She saw no reason why hospital caterers shouldn't take the same care as a fine restaurant and prepare food to order using fresh ingredients. With her staff she developed new menus that included a total of twenty-six choices for breakfast and thirty-two for lunch. The food varied from traditional hamburgers and pizzas to international cuisine such as sushi.

In January 1999 Doherty opened a special outlet for cancer sufferers: the Blossom Street Café. Recognizing that the disease and its treatment often lead to loss of appetite, the café introduced small portions designed to tempt rather than overwhelm their customers. And they didn't forget that patients would be there with their friends and families, so the café catered to them too, with bagels, pastries, salads, and desserts.

By April 1999 the MGH dietetics service was serving a total of nearly nine hundred patients and thirteen thousand nonpatients *each day*. Also in April 1999 Helen Doherty was named Restaurateur of the Year by the Massachusetts Restaurant Association, an award more commonly associated with huge commercial successes like Legal Seafood. Doherty was the first woman and MGH the first institution ever to receive such an award.

Horshin has several important characteristics illustrated by the Sony example:

- It's driven from the top: one key influencer or a very select group of key influencers have to have the drive, the power within the organization, and the vision to push through a horshin change. As chair of Sony, Morita could insist that the company go into production on the Walkman even though all the research said no.
- When an organization makes the leap into a horshin change, it doesn't know exactly where it's going to end up. Morita and the Sony board assumed their target market was people like themselves, yet as we've seen, it wasn't. But Morita, as the horshin driver, insisted that they keep going until they found the true market. Horshin processes are by their nature unstable and uncertain.
- Horshin is followed by kaizen. Since the breakthrough invention of the Walkman, Sony has kept its position as market leader by a process of continuous improvement: reducing the size, improving the quality of the sound, customizing for different groups from tots to teens to middle-aged and elderly businesspeople (even they, in the end, had to come on board). You can't go only for non-stop horshin; it's a tool for creativity, *not* innovation. (We'll be talking more about the distinction between creativity and innovation in the next chapters.)

Horshin Goals: Fighting the Tyranny of Incrementalism

Laurie Gardiner was until recently a regional fundraiser with the National Trust, the United Kingdom's largest NGO, with an income of $160 million. The Trust's mission is to acquire and preserve properties and scenic land for public access.

Laurie had a significant record of achievement in his regional role. But he wanted more. An =mc workshop gave him the inspiration to break out of what he called the tyranny of incrementalism.

He had been given the task of raising around 20 percent of the $7.5 million needed to "buy" from a private owner a Welsh mountain for public use and recreation. He decided to ignore this modest goal and instead aim for the target of raising the whole $7.5 million in just two hundred days. He used the metaphor of a mountain as a way of visualizing and selling his goal.

With a mixture of talent, brains, hard work, and luck, Laurie raised the $7.5 million within the deadline. And the highest and one of the most beautiful mountains in Wales—Mt. Snowdon—was saved for public use.

Examples of Horshin

Some horshin breakthroughs hit the headlines. There are good examples in the world of politics. Take, for instance, German reunification. After some fifty years as a divided country, East and West Germany reunified over the course of a mere nine months. Think too of the sudden growth of Solidarity in Poland following Lech Walensa's famous climb over the wall of the Gdansk shipyard. The fall of Communism is another example: the ideology had been established for seventy years in Eastern Europe, yet all the leading regimes toppled within two years.

And what about the Internet? Invented in the late 1940s as a means of improving communication within the U.S. military, it grew very little outside the military and academic worlds (and not that much in it) for almost forty years. Then, in 1989, an Englishman named Tim Berners-Lee invented a new programming language while working at CERN in Switzerland (Berners-Lee, 2001), which led to the creation of the World Wide Web. This breakthrough piece of programming suddenly made the Internet easy to use. And it took off. Now, according to a presentation we heard at the 2000 Council on Foundations Conference given by the Dell Corporation, there are sixty Web pages for every person *on the planet*. And think of e-commerce. An end-of-millennium spin-off from the Web was the phenomenal rise in dot-com companies. Apparently out of nowhere, they arrived to dominate the stock markets all over the world, pushing some long-established, more traditional companies off the "Top 100 Companies" lists. (And then fell back, of course . . .)

Red Noses and a Million Men

Comic Relief is one of Europe's most successful fundraising charities. Up until 1990 it made money by running a series of well-organized charity concerts and performances attended by important figures in the entertainment world, many of them comedians.

Then their enterprising and visionary CEO, Jane Tewson, had a breakthrough idea: to run an event called Red Nose Day. On this day, she said, millions of people in the United Kingdom would buy and wear a red plastic nose similar to those worn by traditional circus clowns and would do crazy stunts for charity. Many within the organization were initially skeptical. After all, British people are notoriously quiet and reserved. The idea of persuading them to wear a red plastic nose was, frankly, ridiculous.

But Tewson persevered and persuaded the board to support her in arranging to have millions of round red noses made.

Red Nose Day U.K. was a *huge* success. Almost two-and-a-half million noses were sold and worn, raising almost $25 million in the event's first year—the achievement of a horshin vision.

Louis Farrakhan's Million Man March on Washington, D.C., in 1995 was a good example of a horshin phenomenon. It took off from an initial small impulse and then grew in numbers exponentially as black men nationwide decided to commit themselves to the project and the pledge it involved.

Like many horshin phenomena, the "million men" goal was not achieved in strict number terms. It was a visionary and challenging goal, designed to create momentum and excitement.

Advantages of Horshin

What are the *advantages* of horshin?

- A successful horshin leap takes an organization further, in less time, than any other change process.

- For the people on board, it's an exciting and energizing time, bringing with it a real sense of achievement-in-the-making.

- It focuses the organization on its core business: What exactly are we here to achieve? Is it *providing aids for sight-impaired people*, or is it *promoting equality of opportunity for those people* (which might involve a more radical approach)?

- Horshin goals bring with them a can-do attitude not only inside but also outside the organization. The Canadian Diabetes Association, seeing the drive to achieve extraordinary results coming from the NSPCC in the United Kingdom (mentioned in Chapter One), felt inspired to set their own horshin goal "to conquer diabetes."

- As a process, horshin can unleash unlikely champions. Although it's true that the drive will generally come from key influencers and senior people, it can also come from people outside the system, like Tim Berners-Lee. His invention of the World Wide Web was the catalyst for the explosion in Internet usage from the 1990s on.

Disadvantages of Horshin

Let's look now at the disadvantages of horshin:

- It relies on one person—or on a very elite (and small) group of people—to come up with the breakthrough goal or vision and commit to driving it through.

- It generally relies on that person or group to be in a position of power: chief executive, chair of the board, and so on.

- Apart from unusual examples such as the World Wide Web, horshin is usually driven from the top: this can alienate people further down in the organization if they're not convinced about the new direction.

- If the vision or goal isn't "sold" effectively to other people in the organization, they may not come on board and could potentially slow down or even sabotage the process.

- The place where you end up can be so far adrift from the original concept that it can threaten the existence of the organization, or at least challenge its core purpose.

- Horshin goals can look a lot like fantasy at first, especially when they ask for performance improvements of 200 to 300 percent. That element of fantasy can scare people off or cause them to treat the goal as a pipe dream.

Do You Need to Choose Between Horshin or Kaizen?

Many organizations believe they have to choose *either* horshin *or* kaizen, thinking these are incompatible philosophies. In practice, you need to have a mixture of both. Some areas of your work need the stability, methodical progress, and inclusiveness of kaizen. To balance this, you need the drive, transformation, and vision implicit in horshin. An organization could, for example, have ten goals as part of a three-year strategic plan. Of these, probably six or seven will be kaizen; that is, they'll be aimed at incremental improvement toward a significant goal. Three or four might be horshin—that is, areas for rapid change. As an example, the following list shows the goals that are part of the three-year strategic plan of a medical relief charity.

Goals Over Three Years	*Kaizen or Horshin?*
Increase our fundraising from $5 million to $15 million	Horshin
Expand number of medical staff from 350 to 400	Kaizen
Improve ability to recruit and induct new doctors	Kaizen
Improve database to search for diseases	Kaizen

Reduce time to arrive at disaster scene by 10 percent	Kaizen
Expand our operations into sub-Saharan Africa	Horshin
Train more local paramedics over three years	Kaizen
Improve planning process to cope with emergencies	Kaizen

This balance is important. You can't transform everything about your work overnight. You need to focus on and emphasize a small number of key areas to transform quickly.

What's the Difference Between a Horshin Goal and a Mission or Vision?

Sometimes an overarching horshin goal can be exactly the same as a mission or vision. In the case of the NSPCC, "to end child abuse in a generation" and "to increase our fundraising by 300 percent" are almost *missions*. (A *vision* version might be "to create a society in which all children are safe and cared for" or "to ensure we have enough funds to deal with any spending plan we identify.")

More often, though, a horshin goal will be focused around one or more specific areas. In this way they are parallel to kaizen goals. Thus you could create a kaizen or horshin goal in any of the following areas:

- Numbers of people served
- Area served
- Amount of funds raised
- Way of doing business
- Quality of service provided
- Range of services provided

How Can You Tell If a Horshin Idea Is Just a Fantasy?

Obviously anyone can say "Let's double or treble our income" or "Let's get rid of cancer within a year." But are these real goals or simply slogans that are doomed to failure, a failure that might lead to mass alienation from both donors and clients? A *fantasy* is a wild—and attractive!—target, but one without any kind of grounding or focus in reality.

The world of business, politics, and nonprofits is littered with failed or ill-thought-through horshins. For example, a "netfundraising" event supported by Cisco Systems in 1998 and hailed as "Band Aid meets the 21st Century" was the first ever worldwide, webcast-only charity fundraising event. It was designed to reach an audience of two hundred million people logging on to the Internet. The event seemed to have all the right ingredients for horshin: it was supported by top stars like David Bowie and Bono, it had the backing of a leading U.S. company, it tied into the hottest technology—music on the Web. In the end, though, it reached only ten million people and raised just $15.2 million. The horshin leap didn't take off.

Think too of the many dot-com companies that launched in the period between 1999 and 2000. Many of them failed shortly after their flotation or IPO, losing their investors massive amounts of money. They all seemed to have huge potential and supposedly foolproof business plans. But the promise of a massive increase in dot-com income just didn't happen in many cases. (And let's not talk about actual profits.)

Exhibit 3.1 lists six questions you can use to test whether your "horshin" goal qualifies as a real target rather than a fantasy.

Beyond Stretch Goals

The language of planning for results speaks of targets, goals, aims, objectives, step change, and the like. Sometimes people ask if a horshin goal isn't what other people call a stretch goal. The answer is no, it's much more than that. Let's use an analogy.

Look at one of your "horshin" goals and apply these six test questions to determine whether your goal qualifies as a real target rather than a fantasy.

1. Is it *necessary and urgent*—that is, is there an absolute imperative that the goal must be achieved and soon? When people agree that the goal *must* be achieved, their energies and effort become more focused.

2. Can you express it in a *simple and understandable way?* Do people get excited when you describe it? Horshin goals tend to be very straightforward: "to put a man on the moon before the decade is out," "to cure diabetes."

3. Does the goal have a *constituency?* By this we mean, is there a group of people or a powerful individual who owns the goal and feels committed wholeheartedly to its success?

4. Is there a *measure* that will allow you to know you've succeeded? Is there a clear set of metrics for success? Is there a minimum and maximum measure to allow for the vagaries of horshin?

5. Is the goal *demanding* and outside all current industry standards? A 40 percent leap in anything is big, but that could be merely a stretch. Is this goal really extraordinary?

6. Are you and your colleagues prepared to *pay the price* for achieving it? By this we mean that horshin goals often involve sacrifices in other areas of work or personal lives. The question is whether people are prepared to make these sacrifices.

Exhibit 3.1   Is Our Goal Horshin or Fantasy?

Most people see their goals as being like a high jump in athletics. The jumper says, "First, I need to set my high jump goal, based on a reasonable analysis of my past performance. Let's say I set the bar at 1.8 meters. If I achieve that goal, I'll set a new standard 10 percent higher, then train for the new performance level. If I plan my run up and get the timing right for when I take off, I'll clear the 2-meter high jump successfully—I'll achieve my new goal." That's not a bad way to plan for an *incremental* improvement in performance.

Sometimes people are so pleased with their success that they set what they call stretch goals: they raise the bar perhaps 40 or 50 centimeters or some other amount that's a *significant* extension of the current performance. It won't be so straightforward to achieve, but they figure—quite rightly—that if they train harder, take a longer run up, and run faster, they *will* clear the higher bar and so achieve the stretch goal. Stretch goals are useful; they help us move outside the comfort zone to achieve a higher level of performance.

In a nonprofit setting, a stretch goal might involve a 20 percent increase in funds or a 30 percent increase in membership or attendance.

But what happens when you or someone sets the bar *three or four times higher than your current best*, as in Figure 3.3? The tried, tested, and refined techniques just won't work. No matter how much extra training you fit in, no matter how fast you run, it is not physically possible for you to clear the bar at this new extraordinary level using a refinement of the old techniques. In the frame of your current practices the goal may be unreasonable and even seem unachievable. If the goal *is* to be achievable, what's needed is *radical* change: in attitude, in behavior, and in strategy. To jump to the new level of performance shown in Figure 3.3 you're going to have to get seriously creative: use a pole, use a ladder, build an earth mound up to the bar, buy some rocket-propelled shoes, and so on. The breakthrough target *forces* you to think in new radical and creative ways about "how to."

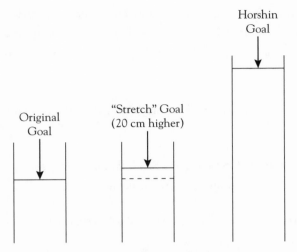

Figure 3.3   Stretch Versus Horshin

They Always Call the New Ideas Crazy . . .

Some readers might remember the 1968 Mexico Olympics where Dick Fosbury, the U.S. athlete, introduced the Fosbury flop in the high jump. His radical backflip technique amazed the spectators and competitors alike. In fact it so astonished the judges that they looked for reasons to disqualify him. But there was nothing in the rule book to say he was acting illegally. He set a new record using it.

Consider, too, the opening night of Mozart's *Marriage of Figaro* in Vienna on May 6, 1789. It was eagerly awaited by the audience, who had enjoyed all his previous operas. But Mozart, ever the innovator, didn't want simply to repeat past successes. In *The Marriage of Figaro* he introduced a number of new ideas and techniques, including having, at one point, six singers singing different words to the same tune. Nowadays it's a familiar technique, but in Mozart's time it was as radical and uncomfortable as an atonal piece by Stockhausen is for many people today.

As you might expect, people hated the opera. The performance broke up in disarray. But Mozart held on to his vision, refusing to change his approach, and gradually people came to love the new opera.

As the famous graffito, attributed to Marshall McLuhan among others, said,

> *In the Kingdom of the Blind, the one-eyed man*
> *is regarded as a hallucinating lunatic.*

You need to expect negative feedback when striving for a real horshin goal.

How to Describe a Horshin Goal

Notice that we are probably not that *excited* by kaizen goals, such as those described here:

- Improve our fundraising target by 7.55 percent.
- Reduce child mortality by 3 percent over ten years.
- Reduce HIV infection rates by a factor of .75 percent.
- Have our theatre reviewed positively by the *New York Times*.

Yes, these goals are purposeful, but they are not exciting and challenging. Notice, though, that we may not get all that excited and engaged by horshin goals that are described merely in terms of bigger numbers:

- Improve our fundraising target by 300 percent.
- Reduce child mortality by 50 percent in five years.
- Reduce HIV infection rates by a factor of 75 percent.
- Have our theatre performances receive rave reviews by 20 percent of major theatre critics.

Clearly, horshin goals need to be described differently. To be truly exciting and involving, they must connect strongly to the right brain: the part of our brain that deals with emotional, visual, creative, and even musical data. Thus you might express the goal as a picture, a feeling, or even a sound. Ideally you can create an effective metaphor for the result or goal and possibly even for the process. For example, we were working with the CEO of a large European cultural NGO with many semi-autonomous branches. The CEO announced his change proposals to colleagues as "the train that's leaving the station." His colleagues understood the metaphor: get on board or get left behind.

As another example, Jubilee 2000 was the worldwide movement dedicated to reducing the burden of debt imposed on developing countries by the industrialized world. Ann Pettifor, director of Jubilee 2000 U.K., asked us to work with her on a breakthrough goal for the G8 Summit in Okinawa. She was going there with a number of colleagues to gain publicity for the cause. Eventually she came up with a promotion horshin goal: "to put poverty on the cover of *Time* magazine." That gave her a vision to orient her behavior and the campaign. She worked with her team to "see" that cover of the magazine as a reality, helping them understand what would and wouldn't get on the cover. (For example, a report wouldn't get on the cover, but a powerful image of a person or group would.)

An engaging horshin goal is more likely to stimulate us in a range of ways. John F. Kennedy's declaration in 1961 that "This nation should commit itself to achieving the goal, before this decade is out, of landing a man on the moon and returning him safely to earth" captured the imagination not only of the American public but also of people all over the world.

There are commercial examples galore. One of the most powerful is Henry Ford's goal or vision for the Ford Motor Company (quoted in O'Keefe, 1998, p. 46): "My vision is to build a motor car for the great multitude. It will be at so low a price that no man making a good salary will be unable to own one. With his car he will enjoy, with his family, the blessing of hours of pleasure in God's great open spaces. The horse will have disappeared from our highways and the automobile will be taken for granted."

Notice the characteristics of this vision:

- It's *concrete* rather than abstract—"at so low a price that no man making a good salary will be unable to own one."
- It's not about sales or markets. It's about *people doing things*.
- It paints a *very specific picture*, yet one that you can put yourself in—"the horse will have disappeared."
- It's clear what *will be the case* and what *will not be the case*.
- It's in simple language, and the proposition is simple, though we know the process will be difficult.

Ford's vision shares many of these characteristics with Martin Luther King Jr.'s famous speech at the Lincoln Monument in 1963. King doesn't say, "I have some key success factors" or "There are some statistical measures of discrimination I'd like to share." He tells us that he has a dream and then paints that dream as a series of vivid, concrete pictures—many of which are meant metaphorically. For example, King talks about the state of Alabama where he wants all children of whatever race to be able to walk together. And he talks about a metaphorical check that must be paid to black people.

Many nonprofits try to take this process further and summarize their mission as an overarching, simple, concrete horshin goal. Some succeed better than others. Here are some real examples:

- "To ensure no child goes to bed hungry" (UNICEF)
- "To end child abuse within a generation" (NSPCC)
- "To find a cure for diabetes" (Canadian Diabetes Association)
- "Drop the debt" (Jubilee 2000)

Horshin goals can also be more specific. Here are some we've made up or adapted from real organizations:

- "To triple our income within three years in order to save the rainforest"
- "To become the largest membership organization in the U.S. supporting the needs of young people"
- "To improve our customer care, so we become the Nordstrom of the nonprofit sector in the U.S."
- "To become a world-class center for research of childhood diseases and to radically reduce their incidence"

Summary

To achieve breakthrough, it can help if you use different language. The language is important because it helps people

- Shift into a different mind-set.
- Distinguish breakthrough goals from ordinary goals.
- Begin to think creatively about "how to" as well as "what."

One example of new language for new ideas that we find useful is a pair of Japanese words:

Kaizen: continuous, incremental improvements toward a breakthrough goal

Horshin: sudden breakthrough and transformation in performance

Kaizen is not the same as incrementalism. Incrementalism is about reviewing the past and trying to identify a small improvement based on that back-projection. Kaizen is about identifying a powerful future goal and taking positive action steps toward it.

As well as conveying different ideas, these words involve different methods and processes. Kaizen is bottom-up and slower. Horshin is top-down and sudden.

You must distinguish between horshin and fantasy. A fantasy is interesting and exciting but not "doable." Horshin is interesting and exciting *and* doable if other factors change.

Action

- Review your current organizational goals. How many are kaizen and how many horshin? How many are incremental and how many fantasy?
- If you don't have any real horshin goals, set some! Make them visceral and alive. Create a picture or metaphor that encompasses them and shows the difference you'll make.
- When you are writing horshin goals, test them by asking yourself, Are they . . .

  Necessary and urgent?

  Simple?

  Measurable?

  Owned?

  Demanding?

  "Costed" in terms of the potential negative consequences both for the organization and the individuals in it?

Note

1. http://www.mgh.harvard.edu/DEPTS/pubaffairs/Issues /Apr30HelenDoherty.htm

Chapter Four

Unlocking Potential

The Strategic Role of Creativity and Innovation

This chapter looks at the ways in which we can unlock our potential through two distinct but linked processes: creativity and innovation. We'll introduce you to six simple rules or techniques that, if applied consistently, will help you achieve *systematic* creativity—that is, the ability to be creative *on demand*.

Creativity and Innovation

If we are to make a breakthrough, it will almost certainly come from doing something different or doing things differently. To make either of these changes we need to be able to think in new ways, which involves both creativity and innovation. As we mentioned, these processes are linked, but it is very important to understand the distinction between them.

Creativity is the process of generating ideas. It involves divergent and random thinking, and mixing up a range of possibilities. By its nature it's chaotic. Creativity produces lots of possibilities, only a small number of which have real potential. This means you must accept that creativity will also produce a great many useless ideas for every one worth running with.

> *The creative act uncovers, shuffles, and changes reality.*
> —Arthur Koestler, 1964

Innovation is the process of choosing and selecting one or more of the ideas generated in creativity mode so as to exploit their potential. It involves convergent and focused thinking. It is systematic and

73

selective. Innovation is rational and organized, and by its nature *practical*. Its outcome is to produce a workable solution, so the starting point is to discard useless ideas.

As individuals and organizations, we need to practice the processes of both creativity and innovation until they become deeply embedded skills. By using *both* of them we can dramatically improve performance, but they do need to be linked and sequenced correctly. Creativity by itself *can* end up as mere indulgence. Ideas just for their own sake may be interesting but often have no use in the real world. Equally, a relentless pursuit of innovation by itself can lead to staleness as the same basic idea is simply recycled and improved. (Or worse still, the wrong idea is pursued.) Organizations have to get this mix of creativity and innovation right. (Chapter Eight further discusses the balancing of creativity and innovation.)

When Innovation Goes Only So Far

Everyone has heard of Wells Fargo. For over half of the nineteenth century, it was the firm that transported people and letters across America. Its fastest time was twenty days to travel from St. Joseph, Missouri, to Sacramento. For West Coast bankers keen to have information on financial transactions this was too long. They were desperate for something quicker.

On April 3, 1860, three visionary men launched the Pony Express with six hundred horses chosen for their speed and seventy-five men selected for their toughness. At a stroke, the journey time was cut in half to just ten days—a horshin achievement for crossing eighteen hundred miles. Their secret was more staging posts, excellent horses, and even asking that letters be written on tissue-thin paper to keep the weight down.

All in all, the Pony Express is an amazing example of innovation and improvement on the Wells Fargo system. What the company didn't count on was the arrival of the electric telegraph. Just twenty months after its inception, the Pony Express was yesterday's technology. Pony Express probably took horse-carried information as far and as fast as it could go. But the telegraph was a radically different and successful creative leap.

Obviously organizations and individuals need both creativity *and* innovation to achieve a breakthrough. There are a whole host of benefits—again, for organizations *and* individuals—in gaining skills in both.

Organizations need these skills in order to

- Create an attractive workplace
- Keep ahead of the competition
- Find new ways to tackle issues
- Avoid stagnating
- Improve the "brand" of the nonprofit
- Build supporter and donor confidence
- Keep funds flowing in
- Create a "can-do" culture
- Attract and retain good staff and board members

Everything on this list is important, but increasingly we're finding that the last benefit is key. Nonprofits are using a reputation for creativity and innovation as a way of attracting board members and, more particularly, staff. The reality is that if you can't pay the highest salaries, then it is this reputation that will help you attract and retain good people.

Individuals need innovation and creativity so as to

- Feel empowered
- Build their confidence
- Overcome personal self-limiting beliefs
- Make work enjoyable
- Feel OK about working long hours
- Feel they're making a difference

- Compensate for a salary lower than they might make in the private sector

All these reasons fit in effortlessly with classic theories of motivation, such as those of Maslow and Hertzberg. These gurus argue that among the highest motivators for people are feelings of self-fulfillment and the sense of being valued. Creativity and innovation are important ways for people to achieve these feelings.

Get Creative

Many people get nervous at this point because they want to say, "But I'm not creative" or "I never have ideas." Our work suggests that

- *Everyone* is creative (and innovative).
- We all have differing *degrees* of creativity (and innovativeness).
- We all have different *styles* and approaches to creativity (and innovation).

Having said that, our experience demonstrates that

- We can all learn to be *skillful* in "turning on" creativity (and innovation).

There's a very simple test to find out just how creative you are right now. All you need is a piece of paper, a pen or pencil, and a watch or timer. Try this. Think of a bottle, any bottle. Now take *exactly* 120 seconds to list as many uses as you can think of for the bottle. The uses can be "normal," wild, wacky, or whatever. Remember, you're trying to be *creative*, so *any* answer counts and is fair. What's important is the *number* of uses you come up with. Because we're not at the moment concerned with innovation, your responses don't have to be *useful*. Begin whenever you're ready.

Once you've finished, add up your "uses," then divide that number by two (for example, 7 answers ÷ 2 = 3.5).

How did you do? The list below shows the rough distribution of how many ideas people come up with (divided by two) in two minutes.

0–3: 5 percent

3–6: 60 percent

6–8: 20 percent

8–10: 10 percent

10–18: 5 percent

No one has ever scored more than 17!

The list is based on running this simple test in countries as diverse as Argentina, Ethiopia, Canada, and Brazil. The distribution of results—a crude measure of creativity we'll admit—is the same across cultures, ages, and professions. Most people score in the 3–6 range, and 95 percent of people score under 10. To improve the score in this and similar tests, you need to improve your systematic creativity—that is, your ability to turn on ideas on demand. That's what this chapter is about.

So let's summarize. If you scored between 3 and 6, you're "normal"—that is, you scored about the average for the population. This is where 60 percent of people score before they've been trained to be systematically creative. This is a good score, because you can build from here.

If you scored more than 6, you're *more* creative than normal. (The highest score ever was 17, achieved by someone at a Mexico City workshop we ran in 1998. This score means that the person came up with thirty-four ideas in two minutes.) If you're in this range you already have an advantage.

If you scored less than 3—fantastic! You have a huge opportunity to make a personal horshin breakthrough in your level of creativity. Keep reading this book.

Rules for Systematic Creativity

So we've agreed it's important to be creative, and you have an idea of how creative you are. But how can you *improve* your creativity—that is, your ability to come up with lots of possibilities? What's needed is not odd flashes of inspiration but systematic creativity, creativity that can be switched on and off like a tap when you need it.

There are six rules for on-tap creativity. To put it more accurately, we will call these *key principles* that we can observe and apply so as to be creative on time, every time:

Key Principles for Achieving Systematic Creativity

1. Go for a "burst."
2. Watch for your preferences.
3. Rule out nothing.
4. Avoid killer phrases.
5. Build on ideas.
6. Look through others' eyes.

The next sections go into more detail on each of these. Please note that you don't necessarily follow these principles in a *sequence*.

Rule 1: Go for a "Burst"

The bottle exercise illustrates two aspects of creativity. One is that you need a stimulus—a provocation, a problem, an object, or whatever—to get the creative juices going. The second is that in order to ensure that you end up with at least *one* good idea you need to have *a lot* of ideas to start with. We call the combination of these two aspects a *burst*—a quick, stimulated, frenetic generation of ideas. This is often referred to as a brainstorm, but a brainstorm may lack the focus or provocation that is *key* to creativity.

The stimulus can be weird and unconnected to the problem you're working on, or it can be wholly associated. For example, if you were a housing advice center trying to find a way to deal with poor housing, you might choose to begin by asking, "What can we learn about good housing from an art gallery [an unconnected stimulus]?" You might come up with answers like these:

- People like to be in attractive surroundings.
- Not everyone thinks the same things are attractive—not everyone likes the same art.
- We could use community artists to improve housing.
- Why shouldn't people be able to choose the color of their houses as artists choose colors for their canvas?
- Why not have sculptures in spaces between houses?

Alternatively, you might choose a more "regular" stimulus, such as "What can we learn from health clinics?" You might end up with these responses:

- Housing needs to promote good health—mental and physical.
- We could give people "prescriptions" to get their house fixed.
- We could dedicate some times for no-appointment drop-ins so that people with a housing emergency can always be seen.
- We should have both "generalist" housing advisers, similar to GPs, and specialists—for example, in housing people with disabilities—like oncologists in a hospital.

Stimuli for creativity can be as diverse as a word, a concept, or, as shown here, another organization. They can be *connected*, as in the housing advice center example, or seemingly *disconnected*, as in the bottle example. They can even be about the idea of *qualities*. For example, you might ask, "How can we use the idea of romance [a strong relationship] to improve our customer/donor relations?" Or you can use organizations you respect: "How would Microsoft or the army or Nordstrom or . . . tackle this problem?"

Art Gallery Goes Popular

We were working with a famous contemporary art gallery in London that wanted to become more attractive to "ordinary" people, recognizing that contemporary art tended to attract a more elitist or educated audience. We began with two bursts. For burst one we asked, "What organizations do 'ordinary' people feel comfortable in?" They came up with a list of twenty, including McDonald's, pubs, Harvester Inns (the TGI Friday's of the United Kingdom), Disneyland, and Hard Rock Cafés. (Notice that many of these places were eating places and that the list, at least in our view, betrayed a certain lack of understanding of "ordinary" people.)

Anyway, we chose the Hard Rock Café (HRC) as the second stimulus. This was not a popular choice, as many of the academic curating staff thought HRC was very downmarket. (We chose it *deliberately* as a venue diametrically opposite in style to the gallery—another provocation.) So for burst two the question was, "How would HRC run this gallery?" Again, the participants came up with a list of twenty ideas, including the following:

- They would structure the gallery materials in clusters like starters, middles, and desserts.
- They'd have "greeters" who say hello and make you feel welcome when you come in.
- Even if they personally disliked the art you wanted to see, the staff would be positive about your choice.
- The staff would wear informal or casual uniforms and would be positively looking for people to help.
- The staff would see it as their job to encourage you to see more art, building and expanding on your appetite (like having another course at HRC).

If you ever visit this famous gallery, you will be greeted when you come in. If one of the informally dressed staff members sees you studying a painting, he or she will come up and say something like "If you like X, there's more of his work on the second floor" or "If you like X, you might want to go and see the exhibition on the third floor."

So when you are going for burst, you are trying to get as many ideas out as quickly as you can, without qualifying or querying suggestions. Don't worry about whether the ideas are sensible. And always use a focus or stimulus to help you. We love the quotation from Leonardo da Vinci here. It carries some of our message about the role of focus and direction in allowing real creativity.

Small rooms discipline the mind. Large rooms distract it.

—Leonardo da Vinci

Rule 2: Watch for Your Preferences

Review your bottle list and choose your favorite idea. Take a moment to think about *why* it appeals to you. Is it because it's funny, because it's eco-friendly, because it's romantic, or what? Make a note of why you like your choice best.

If you were to do the bottle exercise with five other people so as to produce one huge list, then ask each person which was his or her favorite idea, you'd probably find that everyone would select different ideas, for different reasons. You might even find the others' choices bizarre or at least curious. That's because we all have *preferences* for a particular type of creativity or approach to creativity. This preference *can* mean that we sometimes don't value others' creativity as much as we could.

For example, in the bottle exercise, someone might suggest "use as a rolling pin for pastry"—*quite* creative. Someone else might write "use as rocket ship for ants"—*wildly* creative. You could find that when working with colleagues, you prefer the "zany" or "weird" ideas and are less responsive—consciously or unconsciously—to practical, but nevertheless creative, ones. Or the reverse might be the case. You may prefer the semipractical ideas and dismiss off-the-wall ones.

Or you might find it difficult to come up with politically incorrect or user-unfriendly or unecological uses.

To be successful in creativity you have to be open to *all* kinds of ideas, even ones you don't like. That's why Rule 2 is Watch Out for Your Preferences. The equally important corollary to this rule is Be Aware of Others' Preferences and Value Them. Whatever your preferences, they can lead you to value some ideas more than others too early in the process and so close down your own or others' creativity.

Rule 3: Rule Out Nothing

Now try a third experiment. Still working with the bottle, take sixty seconds to write down uses it *could not possibly be put to*.

You may have noticed that as you began to try to write down some impossible things, you suddenly thought, "In fact, you *could* do that with a bottle." If you were to add those "extra" ideas to your original set of possible uses, the list would of course be longer. Perhaps you would have achieved an *above average* score!

The point is, we all close down ideas too soon, and that limits our creativity. We limit our potential to come up with possible breakthrough solutions by putting up filters. That's what you probably did in the first pass of the bottle test: you prefiltered ideas. Notice, too, that "Come up with impossible ideas" is a burst technique. By thinking of the impossible we actually realize what is possible.

Having said that, however, you probably did write down some things that you still think are impossible. To follow Rule 3, Rule Out Nothing, means that we should try to use creativity to make *everything* possible. Look at Table 4.1 to see how we've made some supposedly impossible ideas possible by applying *creativity*. In these examples, we've begun by casting off some limitations about bottles.

Notice that in our list we haven't made assumptions that all bottles have to be made of glass or plastic or be of a certain size. Indeed, for those of you who said a bottle couldn't be used for clothing, Gore-Tex®—the weatherproof savior of outdoor enthusiasts the

Table 4.1   The Impossible Made Possible

Impossible Idea	How to Do It
Use a bottle as a friend.	Ask the bottle for advice and spin it with various options marked out on a piece of paper. Do whatever the bottle points to.
Use a bottle for a retirement pension.	Collect enough bottles—3 million?—and cash them in for the deposit. Or melt them down and make high-quality glassware you can sell.
Use a bottle as a food source.	Have a bottle made of bread or chocolate. Then you can eat it. (Or glass might make good roughage!)
Use a bottle to travel to the moon.	The Saturn rockets used in the U.S. Apollo space program were really just giant bottles filled with liquid propellant . . .
Use a bottle to reduce stress.	Take deep breaths through your nose and blow out slowly through your mouth across the top of a glass bottle. Slowed breathing combined with musical sound will reduce stress.

world over—is made from recycled plastic bottles. (The learning for the art gallery we described earlier was that one needn't limit one's perception of what an art gallery is like—assuming, for example, that it's a place where the paintings are hung in chronological order or where the staff have to "protect" the paintings or where only certain types of people go.)

There are some really simple techniques at work here to help make the impossible possible. Table 4.2 on page 84 shows five of the most common.

Let's look at some examples of these techniques at work. Historically a number of people have used one or more of the tactics to solve an apparently intractable challenge. Take the "reversal" technique. For three thousand years, bridges had been built on the arch principle. This method worked, but it limited the width of river or

Table 4.2   Five "Make It So" Tactics

"Make It So" Tactic	How It Works
Reverse	Try to look at whatever it is the other way around—the opposite
Change size	Would it help if you made the frame of reference bigger or smaller?
Change material	Would it help if you changed the material you used?
Change numbers up or down	Would it make a difference if you had a much bigger or smaller number?
Add to or take away	Could you add something to the thing to make it so?

gap the bridge could cross in a single span. In the eighteenth century, Isambard Kingdom Brunel "flipped over" in his mind a traditional arch bridge and invented and built the first suspension bridge, in Bristol, England. This reversal led to a revolution in bridge building. Without it there would be no Golden Gate Bridge connecting San Francisco to Marin County.

In South Africa, the Truth and Reconciliation Commission reversed the basic principle of a traditional court of justice. Normally courts work by determining whether a defendant is telling the truth and punishing him or her if the individual is found guilty. Clearly in this system it's not in a guilty defendant's best interest to tell the truth.

For South Africa, at this time, it was more important for people to know the truth about what had been going on in the years of apartheid—what had happened to the relatives who had disappeared, where bodies could be found and given a proper burial. So instead of saying to the defendants, "Tell the truth and we'll punish you if you are found guilty," the court said, "If you *don't* tell the truth—all of it, however heinous—we will punish you. If you *do* tell the truth, you will be pardoned." This reversal led former Archbishop Desmond Tutu to agree to chair the commission. The work of the commission, in the opinion of many in the country, has helped bind South Africa together.

A last example: U.S. scientists are working on using the AIDS virus to tackle cancer, seeing it not as an enemy but as a powerful weapon able to adapt and change radically.

The "add to" principle, as the name suggests, involves adding to the basic idea. You may remember the story of the surgeon who saved a woman with a collapsed lung on a long-haul flight. He had no surgical equipment with him and had to work with what the airline could provide: a scalpel, a plastic water bottle, some tubing, and plenty of alcohol to act as a disinfectant. Using these, he put together a tube-and-bottle system that allowed her lung to inflate and saved her life.

If you're a soft contact lens user, you probably remember a time when to clean your lenses you first had to put them in a solution, then add a revitalizing tablet, and so on. Then someone thought of adding to the bottom of the lens case a fixture coated with the revitalizer, so that as soon as you put your lenses into the cleansing solution the revitalizer also starts. It's a classic example of the "add to" approach.

Rule 4: Avoid Killer Phrases

We all use killer phrases—that is, phrases that have the effect of depressing our own or others' creativity. They may discourage people from challenging accepted wisdom and force them to work inside the box. We don't necessarily mean them to have that effect, but they are nevertheless often used in meetings to put down or crush a new idea. A creative idea is like the young shoot of a plant; it's not really mature enough to stand on its own in the frost of rational analysis. The main concern is that if you crush the new shoot of an idea too soon, you'll never know if it was destined to be a weed or a flower. Some examples of killer phrases are "It'll never work here," "The board won't stand for it," and "It's not in the budget." No doubt you can think of some killer phrases you've heard—or even used yourself.

We're not suggesting that you *never* use these phrases. At least some of them are useful in the innovation phase when you *want* to exclude nonworkable ideas so as to select the best ones. We are suggesting that when you want to be in *creative* mode, such phrases should be avoided.

A team at the Charities Aid Foundation (CAF) in the United Kingdom has formally banned killer phrases in its creativity meetings. If anyone utters one of them, that person has to wear a plastic dagger "through" his or her head for one minute, write the banned phrase on a card, and pay a fine. This is oddball behavior from an organization famous for its conservatism, but it's vital in helping the people there change the way they do things.

Rule 5: Build on Ideas

It's not enough just to stop stifling ideas. You need to positively *build* on ideas to help them flourish, to make them happen. In fact, one good, workable idea often emerges from the combining of two others.

This technique has a long and illustrious history. For instance, take Johannes Gutenberg, the fifteenth-century inventor of the first printing press with moveable type. The idea of the press evolved from a trip he had made into town where he had observed, first, a wine press crushing grapes and, second, the process of using metal dies to stamp out coins. Gutenberg took the two ideas and combined them to come up with a printing press: an adapted wine press with moveable type made from lots of small, die-cast letters. This was the start of the mass production of books, and it remained the dominant printing technology for the next six hundred years until the arrival of digital printing in the late twentieth century. It was a breakthrough—horshin—leap from two well-established kaizen processes. It also combined two apparently *disconnected* ideas.

The Build on Ideas rule involves putting together two unlikely concepts and seeing what the product of these might be. In the upcoming section on mind tiles, we'll talk about how to do this *systematically*.

Rule 6: Look Through Others' Eyes

The last key creativity technique is to look through others' eyes, to experience and make use of their perception of events or activities. This approach is especially useful for organizations trying to become more customer- or client-focused.

There's an example from the business world that contains valuable learning for nonprofits, whatever field they work in. It concerns the success of a famous jewelry retailer in the United Kingdom, Gerald Ratner. In the 1980s he built his business up very quickly, beginning as a small operation and becoming the largest jeweler in Britain. He sold low-cost jewelry—a notoriously low-margin, highly competitive business.

Ratner attributed his success to one simple idea. When he first took over the company, he realized that all the windows of his shops—like those of his competitors—had been designed and built by men. He knew that the vast majority of his customers were women and that they were, on average, four inches shorter than those men. Trying to look in the windows from a woman's height, he noticed that the displays were at a slightly awkward angle and therefore difficult to see clearly. His solution was to lower the bottom edge of all his retail shop windows by four inches—a hugely expensive operation to display the jewelry at a height that suited women. But the result was an extraordinary 15 percent increase in profits wherever the windows were altered.

As we said, the Look Through Others' Eyes technique is equally valuable for nonprofits. One outstanding example of its application is at the prestigious National Gallery in London. The gallery has no entrance fee, so Colin McKenzie, the head of development, was keen to increase the amount of money the gallery earned from the voluntary donation boxes placed just inside the entrance. He decided to focus on how people experienced one specific box. At that time the gallery brought in around $105,000 a year from that box. After hearing of the Ratner example, McKenzie decided to spend a morning studying how people experienced and used (or didn't use) the box. He himself walked past it a number of times trying to see it through visitors'—potential donors'—eyes. He watched other people coming in. From his intuitive and creative research he concluded that he didn't need to change the box's shape or size, or to do anything complex. But he did do one simple thing: he had it moved just fifteen feet to *outside* the entrance. The gallery's income from the donation box went up by more than a factor of three to $345,000 a year, a *massive* increase in income. Colin's genius was simple:

- He looked through others' eyes and invested enough time to do it properly.

- He observed that once visitors were inside the gallery, there were a lot of exciting signs directing them to the gallery's treasures, so the box for money was having to work very hard.

- He showed a crucial understanding of psychology when he concluded that once people were in the gallery they felt they were *entitled* to use it. By moving the box outside, he made people feel they should contribute to gain the right to come in.

To use the Look Through Others' Eyes technique, begin by thinking about whose eyes to look through. Here are some examples:

- Your customers or users
- Members of "excluded" communities who do not currently use your services
- Your competitors
- Your funders
- An organization you admire
- Board members and junior staff

Table 4.3   Looking Through Others' Eyes

Whose Eyes Should We Look Through?	What Barriers Might They See or Experience?	How Could We Reduce These?	Where Do These People Feel Most Wanted?	How Could We Model That?
Board members	• They don't have enough information about what we do. • They've never done our jobs.	• Give each a laptop with online access. • Have a job-shadowing program: each board member shadows a staff member for a month.	• In their own business. • In their own home.	• Have a board meeting in people's businesses. • Ask them to bring their family along to a board meeting.

The second part of the technique is trying to imagine what it's like to be a member of that group or how he or she might perceive what's going on. This process, of course, is used by disability awareness trainers. They may ask you to get to work in a wheelchair, try to use the computer or telephone with frosted glasses that simulate sight impairment, or wear headphones through which muffling sounds are being played and then try to follow a conversation to experience what it's like to have a hearing impairment.

Table 4.3 models a Look Through Others' Eyes exercise you can apply to your organization.

Mind Tiles: Bringing the Six Rules of Creativity Together

There's a process that combines all six rules for creativity in an energizing collective activity: it's called mind tiles, and we've used it extensively in organizational idea-generating problem solving. The basic principle behind mind tiles is very straightforward: you try to

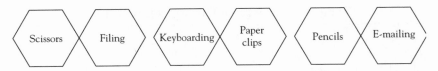

Figure 4.1   Mind Tiles, Step Two

create a third idea by building on a combination of two others. At its simplest, you make a new product from two existing ones. Gutenberg's printing press, for example, came from combining *wine press* with *die-cast coins*.

Here's an example. Imagine you wanted to come up with a new office product. The first step is to make two lists of office *products* and office *activities*:

Office Products	*Office Activities*
Scissors	Filing
Post-it® notes	Keyboarding
White-out liquid	E-mailing
Paper clips	Writing
Pencils	Thinking

You then write each product and each activity two or three times on separate "tiles"—large colored Post-its are ideal. In step two you put these together in a random way, as shown in Figure 4.1.

Depending on how many products and activities you started with, and by repeating tiles to increase the number of possible permutations, you could end up with a whole wall filled with these random connections. Let's imagine you have such a wall. In step three, as a group you add a third tile that conceptually and physically connects the two other tiles. You write on this third tile your idea for a new product, as shown in Figure 4.2. This makes a conceptual, creative connection.

So what kind of ideas can you create from the random juxtaposition of *scissors* and *filing*? How about

- The filing shredder: a shredder that sits by the side of a filing

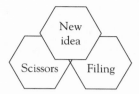

Figure 4.2   Mind Tiles, Step Three

cabinet so you're encouraged to think, "Do I *need* to file this, or should I just shred it?"

- Self-shred paper: paper that automatically shreds itself after two years so that you simply empty your filing cabinet of useless paper.

Let's try another combination: *paper clips* and *keyboarding.* How about a special key on a keyboard that instructs a laser printer to staple or paper clip documents together? You get the idea.

As a group, you work your way across the whole wall of ideas looking to make various contributions. The reason you have more than one version of each combination is because you may well come up with more than one idea for a specific combination.

It's important to remind you here that 99 percent of the ideas gathering on the wall at this point will be *terrible*—or at least not *practical.* But they're creative ideas, and you need only one good one from the whole wall . . .

It's easy to see how mind tiles can be a stepping stone to new products, but you can use it in other ways too:

- You can use just one "stimulus" word to see how it can apply to a whole range of ideas you want to explore. For example, put up all your current services on individual tiles and then add a tile with the one word *Internet* on it to each. On the third tile you're then looking for a solution to the question, "How could we use the Internet to improve this service?"
- You can write your organizational goals on one set of tiles and on another set put the names of individuals or teams. In this

case the third tile answers "How can this person or team contribute to the goal?" So you have *Mabel Smith*, receptionist, on one tile and *build the strategic plan* on another. You're looking for empowerment ideas.

There are eight simple rules to make the mind tiles exercise work:

1. Use a big wall.
2. Have lots of "tiles" made or use big Post-its.
3. Play music while people do the exercise—ideally upbeat! Music stimulates the right side of the brain and thus helps people come up with ideas.
4. Make sure everyone *stands* while they do it—again, this enhances creativity.
5. Use different colored pens—flipchart pens are good—to write on the tiles.
6. Ensure that no one makes comments that indicate mind-sets or judgments on the combinations; the point is to have *lots* of ideas.
7. Do the exercise fairly quickly—in five minutes or less. The burst effect works best in a short time span.
8. Have a clear *purpose*: "Let's come up with new ways to involve users in planning," "Let's try to come up with a new fundraising idea."

The mind tiles technique has been used many times by nonprofits. For example:

• A Canadian recycling charity used mind tiles to combine its current fundraising techniques with a new stimulus. The staff wrote everything they did to raise money onto Post-it tiles, including special events, planned giving, legacies, static collection boxes, phone-a-thons, and so on. They had about twenty to twenty-five techniques. Then they combined each of these techniques with a second Post-it tile on which were written products that had once been successful but were now unfashionable and so suitable for recycling (examples included hula hoops, loon pants, eight-track cartridges, slide rules, and Tamagochis, the small electronic "pets" that were popular with children five or six years ago). Most of the combinations were judged in the innovation phase to be useless or impractical for various reasons. But one—*static collection boxes* and *Tamagochi*—produced the idea of Tamagochi collection boxes. This idea flew. The organization contacted the Tamagochi company and asked for a donation of the computer chips that made Tamagochis interactive. The Tamagochi company was happy to recycle the "useless" chips, and the charity now had a collection box that had an integrated LED display in the form of an electronic "pet." If you didn't give the pet attention by putting in money, it would whimper and look unhappy on the screen. If you put money in, it showed it was happy and collected "goods" from a charity store to distribute.

Using the same technique, a cancer charity came up with the idea of online wills by combining *wills* and *Internet* on two tiles.

Summary

Creativity is something everyone can do. More important, you can do it *systematically*, so that it's available when you need it. But we all need to work at it.

We've given you six rules to apply. Some of them might seem counterintuitive to you (that's because they don't fit in with your preferences, but they might fit perfectly with others'). We assure you that they are all tried and tested principles.

As is true of everything else, you need to work at creativity to get better. Our experience suggests that by applying these six rules you can ensure that any group you're leading in a creativity session will produce *more* ideas. And if you produce *more*, there's a better chance that you'll get one or more *useful* outcomes in the innovation phase explored more fully in Chapter Nine.

Don't be obsessed with the *one* good idea. Most good ideas are hybrids. Look for opportunities to *combine* ideas to make a better one. This also promotes group creativity.

Action

Think about an issue you need to take action on—one for which your current thinking isn't providing any real solutions. Now think of a way to organize a burst to tackle it. You could organize the burst by using a single focus or provocation. For example,

- What could we learn from another organization on how to tackle this challenge? How would the U.S. Marines tackle it?
- How could we gain inspiration from a seemingly irrelevant object on how to deal with this issue—for example, a pen, a brick? (We've got to be tough like a brick. We've got to communicate better like the pen.)

Once you've started this process, work through the other rules as you see fit. For example, Rule Out Nothing could be applied to an environmental charity listing all the companies who make polluting chemicals and whom they would normally attack. Then the environmentalists could ask, "How could we become partners and work with these companies to clean up their act?"

Before you schedule a creativity (burst) session, answer these questions:

- Whom should you ask to be involved?
- When could you have the burst to maximize creativity—morning, afternoon, or evening?
- What complementary stimulus can you add to help switch on the creative process—play music, meet in an art gallery, have "different" food?

Now go for it.

Chapter Five

Releasing Creativity

Unleashing the Power of Your Intelligence

In a situation ripe for breakthrough, people often complain that they don't have enough resources: "If only we had more time," "If only we had a new IT system," "If only we had more money." The reality is that we often can't have more of these kinds of resources. (And even if we could, things wouldn't *necessarily* get better.) This chapter shows how to take advantage of our greatest resource, one we often fail to use properly: our brain. Even a tiny improvement in the use of our brain will give us a huge extra resource.

We'll explore first how to improve your use of the brain's *hardware* so that you're equally comfortable accessing the left (rational) and right (creative) sides of your brain. Then we'll look at multiple intelligences—the brain's *software*—and how we need to use different intelligences to sell and achieve breakthrough.

Your Brain and Everyone Else's

The human brain isn't the largest on the planet; an elephant's weighs five time more. Dolphin brains seem to have a more complex structure. But the human brain does seem to be dominant . . .

The average man's brain weighs 1,390 grams, and women's are about 10 percent lighter. Some brains are heavier: Lord Byron's was an amazing 2,332 grams, Trotsky's was 1,588 grams, and Marilyn Monroe's was 1,440 grams. But there doesn't seem to be a link between size and effectiveness!

Besides weight, there are other significant differences between men's and women's brains. Women tend to be better at language, empathy, and cooperation. They generally see a far wider range and more nuances of color. Men find it easier to rotate objects in their mind's eye and to tackle mathematical problems. They can more accurately guess measurements, whether of distance, width, or area.

A User's Manual for the Brain: Your Potential

The brain is an intensely complex organ, capable of extraordinary achievements. To give you some idea of its potential, consider the number that follows. What do you think it represents?

> 1,000,000,000,000,000,000,000,000,000,000,000,000,
> 000,000,000,000,000,000,000,000,000,000,000,000,
> 000,000,000,000,000,000,000,000,000,000,000,000,
> 000,000,000,000,000,000,000,000,000,000,000,000,
> 000,000,000,000,000,000,000,000,000,000,000,000,
> 000,000,000,000,000,000,000,000

Most people guess that it's the number of brain cells a person has. Not so. It's actually the number of stars in the known universe. It's a big number. Now consider this one:

> 1,000,000,000,000,000,000,000,000,000,000,000,000,
> 000,000,000,000,000,000,000,000,000,000,000,000,
> 000,000,000,000,000,000,000,000,000,000,000,000,
> 000,000,000,000,000,000,000,000,000,000,000,000,
> 000,000,000,000,000,000,000,000,000,000,000,000,
> 000,000,000,000,000,000,000,000,000,000,000,000,
> 000,000,000,000,000,000,000,000,000,000,000,000,
> 000,000,000,000,000,000,000,000,000,000,000,000,
> 000,000,000,000,000,000,000,000,000,000,000,000,
> 000,000,000,000,000,000,000,000,000,000,000,000,
> 000,000,000,000,000,000,000,000,000,000,000,000,
> 000,000,000,000.

This number represents all the possible combinations of synaptic connections your brain is capable of making. That's a lot of processing power. Yet contemporary thinking suggests that we may use only 5 to 10 percent of our capacity at any given time—leaving massive room for improvement. To use an analogy, it's as though you bought a Pentium 4, 1.2 GHz computer and used it only for addition and subtraction. If we were to tap only a *tiny* extra percentage of our brain's power, it would mean we had access to significant extra resources. To achieve breakthrough we need to tap that unused power.

Making a Map: Looking at the Hardware

We're agreed we can all make more use of our brains, but to actually do that we need first to understand how the brain is structured. People have known for hundreds of years that the brain is divided into left and right halves, or hemispheres, and that these hemispheres can work independently and are responsible for different functions. (Even the ancient Romans knew that damage on the right side of the brain could lead to a lack of physical control on the left side of the body.) The two hemispheres are almost separate brains, but they are linked by a network of fibers at the back called the *corpus collosum,* which shares data between them.

The following list outlines what the left and right sides of the brain are *primarily* responsible for. Figure 5.1 is a simple schematic version of the same information.

Left	*Right*
Logic	Intuition
Language	Visual information
Words	Music and rhythm
Short-term memory	Long-term memory
Arithmetic	Creativity
Rational thought	Feelings
Detail	Overview
Data	Synthesis

Figure 5.1   The Two Sides of the Brain

Think of the list and the image in Figure 5.1 together as a sort of topological map to help guide you around the brain. Remember, though, that so-called left- and right-brained activities don't represent an absolute distinction, just as a map of the New York subway system doesn't represent the true distance between stations but rather serves as a way to help you navigate around the subway. And just as a subway map won't help you find a specific apartment in Greenwich Village, our map is only a *general representation* of the relationship between different functions. (Please note, however, that research over the past twenty to thirty years using magnetic resonance imaging [MRI] has brought scientists close to producing a very detailed map of brain function. Already the research has produced some amazing results. For example, it is now known that when schizophrenics hear voices in their heads, their brains actually show patterns similar to those seen when they're hearing genuine external voices. Research has also discovered a place in the brain where humor seems to be processed. By putting a probe into the brain and electrically stimulating that section, researchers can make people laugh and feel cheerful—no joke necessary!)

By understanding the primary functions of the two sides of the brain, we can decide *where* we would like to process information about challenges, ideas, or solutions. It's obvious that in a work setting we tend to use more of the functions that the left brain seems to process: logic and analysis, rational thought, and detail. The left brain is ideal for innovation—turning ideas into workable solutions.

As you might expect, the right side of the brain seems to have strong links to activities related to creativity and imagination. Stimulating the right side of the brain can help you come up with creative ideas. You probably have some experience of this phenomenon, maybe getting big, important ideas as visual images or coming up with a new idea while listening to music.

How to Access the Right Brain: Brain Aerobics

Creativity often comes when we're in a relaxed state, apparently disconnected from the inspiration that is to come. This state of mental relaxation—some call it daydreaming—leads to an increase in the level of certain alpha frequency waves in the brain and to the stimulation of right brain activities. Archimedes made the discovery that led to the formulation of Archimedes' Principle when he realized that the amount of water that overflowed his bathtub was proportional to the amount of his body that was submerged. Einstein's Theory of Relativity came to him in a waking dream that he consciously stimulated by lying on the grass outside his study at Zurich Polytechnic. He wanted to "dream" what it would be like to travel through space at the speed of light. How often have you come up with new and exciting ideas in disassociated situations—in the bath, dozing in the sun, out on a country walk?

If you want to achieve breakthrough by accessing your creativity and gaining new insights, you need to learn how to put yourself quickly into that relaxed mental state and stimulate the right brain. This takes practice. You can't simply sit down at work and say, "Now I'm going to use my right brain to transform my organization." You need to build your skills and flexibility rather as in school and college you had to learn to develop your left brain skills. The following exercises will help get you in shape.

What follows is a list of different warm up activities. You can use them singly or in short sequences before you begin a creativity session, or as a break when you've been exclusively using your left brain.

- Tell a child a story with lots of sound effects, expression, and gestures. Really get into it and make it alive. Tell a work story in the same way . . .
- Study something—a flower or a piece of material, for example—*intensely* for three minutes. Notice as much as you can about it: the color, the texture, the taste, the smell, the various elements and structures in it. Apply that same intensity to a work challenge . . .
- Think back over any dreams or daydreams or fantasies you've had recently and write them down. How did you feel? What did you hear? What did you see? Now use your fantasy skills and revisit your organization's vision . . .
- Try to do an everyday activity, such as brushing your teeth, writing your name, or tying a tie, with your nondominant hand in control. Notice how you need to deconstruct what has until now been natural to you, how you see it in a new light. Now try writing a report in the same way . . .
- Try to remember what it was like when you were four or five years old. Where did you live? What did you do? What did your house look like? What would your four- or five-year-old self have thought about your challenge? How would you have tackled it back then?
- Imagine a smell. Think of the smell of oranges. What does Christmas smell like? Can you remember a perfume your mother used to wear? What does your breakthrough smell like?
- Go for a journey in your imagination—a cycle ride in a park or a walk through a city. Make it as detailed as you can. On your journey, think about arriving at a location where you can solve challenges.

- Try to write down your *feelings* about some event recently. It could be an item in the news or something that happened to you. Now write down your *feelings* about an event at work.

- Choose a song you like. Sing it out loud the way you do when you're in the shower or doing a household chore. Notice how that song makes you *feel*. What song would help you tackle your current work challenge?

- Choose a piece of music you don't know—even a style of music you *don't like*—and listen to it. What images and ideas does it bring to you? Could you use that music to problem-solve?

- Choose a piece of music you do know—Beethoven's Sixth Symphony ("Pastoral"), for example. Create your own version of Walt Disney's *Fantasia* by allowing the music to suggest images and experiences. Are any of those images relevant to your task?

- Take a big piece of blank paper—flipchart size—and lots of colored pens. Make a drawing of your organization as though it were a building. Is it a circus tent, a station, an airport, a castle, or what? What does your drawing tell you about the good things and the things that aren't working in your organization?

- Go back to the burst approach outlined in Chapter Four. You'll find that if you've put in some practice, your mind is a lot looser and freer and that you produce a larger number of ideas.

- Allow yourself to simply dream or drift to see what pops into your head. You can do this consciously in a daydream, or you can try sleeping while considering a challenge and see if you dream a solution.

- Go out on a walk, seeking an external stimulus and a serendipitous answer. Pringles brand potato chips were invented when the food technologist in charge of the development of a new chip went into the park. It was autumn, and it had been raining. He saw a park keeper picking up wet leaves and putting them into bags. The food technologist thought it couldn't be a very pleasant job, and asked the man why he didn't do it when the leaves were dry. "Because they pack more easily when they're wet," came the reply.

The technologist's challenge at that time was to find a way of packing the chips that was economical and that stopped them from breaking before they reached the consumer. The park keeper had given him the answer: stack the chips while they're still wet, then dry them packed together. And that's how Pringles does it (Gordon and Poze, 1987).

Does Serendipity Play a Role in Creativity?

People sometimes argue that the creative process involves serendipity—a fortunate happenstance. Serendipity does indeed have a role. Here are two famous examples from science, often thought of as the most rational of activities.

Alexander Fleming "discovered" penicillin by accident when some bread mold invaded a bacteria culture he had made. He noticed that the mold killed a dangerous bacillus he was growing in the dish. (Note that it was his unsung assistant, Norman Heatley, who worked on the *innovation* part; Heatley was the one who made the substance in enough quantity to have an impact.)

Waldo Semon, a U.S. industrial chemist, was trying to bind metal and rubber in an experiment in 1929. One candidate for the binding agent was polyvinyl chloride (PVC), but it didn't work very well as a glue. It would sit on the surface of the metal or rubber but wouldn't stick to them. In a playful moment—and there is an interesting connection between playful, right-brain thinking and creativity—Semon molded some PVC around a metal ball bearing and noticed that it bounced. It bounced into a bucket of water, and Semon observed that it floated, too. He noted only that this was unusual. He went home, where by chance his wife was sewing a shower curtain. She was using heavy, rubber-coated cotton—the only waterproof material available at the time. Seeing her, Semon suddenly realized that his "useless" PVC might work as a waterproof coating for all kinds of things.

As described in *Newsweek* (Rosenberg, 1997), Semon then set out to sell his idea to a skeptical boss. Taking some PVC-coated material to his boss's office, he put it on top of the paper in the In tray. He then poured a jug of water over it. His astonished boss saw that the papers were dry; he backed the development of the new lighter, cheaper, more malleable substance.

Our Multiple Intelligences: The Software

We've been talking about "unlocking" your hardware to make it more effective. How about the software? Some of the most interesting psychological work carried out in the last five to ten years has focused on the issue of so-called multiple intelligences. The basic idea is simple: we all have access to a number of different ways of processing information, called intelligences.

The original idea of multiple intelligences was developed by Howard Gardner, a Harvard psychologist, in his book *Frames of Mind* (1983). Since then, his basic model of seven intelligences has been extended and adapted by many experts. Some experts, Tony Buzan, for example, reckon we have as many as ten. Daniel Goleman (1995) developed the idea of emotional intelligence (EI), perhaps the best known of the intelligences. Goleman's influential work made EI a key issue for managers and others.

Gardner's Seven Intelligences

Let's look at what the intelligences are and how to use them. There is no definitive list of intelligences, but most experts agree that the seven described by Gardner serve as a good base. The list that follows is a slightly updated and amended version of Gardner's list.

1. *Physical/kinesthetic intelligence:* the ability to process experience through bodily sensations and to coordinate the body and its movements well. If you are strong in this intelligence, you may have always been a fidget as a child, hating to sit still for too long. You

probably have good motor and hand-eye coordination. You may communicate a lot by touch, and learn and solve problems by doing—coming up with a solution by trying something out. Dancers, gymnasts, and sports people often are high in this intelligence, as are sculptors, potters, and carpenters.

2.   *Logical/mathematical intelligence:* the ability to use rational, abstract thought to arrive at logical deductions. As a child, you may have found pleasure in pattern-type games. You may have asked a lot of Why? questions. You like to learn in a structured and organized way. We would expect mathematicians and engineers to be high in this intelligence, but also people with a strong financial background.

3.   *Spatial/visual intelligence:* the understanding of space and of how things will look or appear. You may need things to be "just so" or organized, and you're able to arrange things in neat or appropriate patterns. Builders, artists, and architects are often strong in this intelligence. Think back to the discussion on using mind tiles in Chapter Four. This process is particularly effective for people with strong spatial/visual and physical/kinesthetic intelligences.

Same Problem, Different Solution

We all have access to all the intelligences, but our *ability* to access them and the *amount* we can access them vary. Because of these preferences, different people will choose to use different intelligences to solve the same challenge.

If, for example, you had a broken clock, you could put it back together using visual/spatial intelligence *or* logical/mathematical intelligence. In the first approach, you'd be concerned with how things fit together—does it look right? In the second, you'd want to follow exact instructions.

4.   *Linguistic intelligence:* the ability to use words well or to learn languages easily and fluently. You learn most easily through talking and reading. You may well enjoy playing with words and especially enjoy word games like crosswords. You can probably quote phrases from poems or books. This intelligence is likely to be strong among

writers, journalists, and even translators. This is a very common intelligence among senior managers who can win people over with the quality of their arguments. They may well give outstanding speeches and presentations.

5. *Creative/musical intelligence:* a special kind of creative intelligence—the ability either to make or to appreciate music. You are able to pick out intricate rhythms or to play instruments easily or to identify a style of music. You may well like to have music playing in the background. You probably learn through nonverbal pace and rhythm. An artist or a critic would likely be strong in this kind of intelligence. As a nonprofit manager, you may not use this much at work, but you may find you use music to get you in the mood for creative thinking.

6. *Emotional/interpersonal intelligence:* the ability to empathize with others and to build rapport quickly and easily. You may, in your youth, have been a leader in groups and been seen as streetwise and confident. You have a real gift for sensing how people are and how a group is feeling, and you may be able to manage a group's feelings well. You probably learn best in a group situation. Anyone from managers to salespeople can be strong in this intelligence.

7. *Intrapersonal intelligence:* the ability to be at peace with oneself—to have a calm and balanced approach to life, or to consider bigger issues in more reflective ways. A guru or philosopher or holy person is likely to be highly developed in this intelligence. You may have it if you like to think things through. In an nonprofit setting, people strong in this intelligence may want very much to work from a values or beliefs basis (and not change those values or beliefs easily).

Applying Intelligences

As we've said, it's helpful to think of the intelligences as the brain's software. Like computer programs for spreadsheets, word processing, and presentations, each intelligence does different things. Although we don't want to push the metaphor *too* far, let's continue with the software idea just a bit longer.

Some challenges are best solved using a *specific* intelligence—just as it's easiest to do a budget in Excel. If you don't have easy access to that intelligence, you need to try to develop it or work with someone who has it already. With access to a strong spatial intelligence, for example, you'll find it quite straightforward to work out the office reorganization or to set up the refugee camp.

Some challenges need a *combination* of the intelligences to achieve a result, much like preparing a presentation using Excel *and* Word *and* PowerPoint. Again, you need to learn to use your own intelligences better—or even acquire new ones—*and* to engage your colleagues in using theirs more effectively. So, for example, planning a major fundraising campaign will involve emotional, rational, and linguistic intelligences. You'll even need all of these to write a good appeal letter.

Research suggests that although we all have *access* to all these intelligences at some level, we don't *use* them all with the same facility. So, just as we are left-handed or right-handed, we prefer using some intelligences more than others. Unlike handedness, however, which is fixed, preferences can be modified: we can learn to use more often those intelligences with which we are less naturally comfortable. Of course, it goes without saying that society values certain intelligences more in certain settings. IQ tests, still popular in some educational settings, are tests of only a limited number of intelligences: logical/mathematical, linguistic, and spatial/visual.

In our work, we've found that for individuals or organizations to achieve breakthrough, they need to use a *range* of these intelligences.

The Multi-Intelligence Breakthrough

Suppose the CEO of a women's refuge wants to sell the idea of a new refuge to her board or funders. To improve her chances of success, she can make her pitch in a number of ways so as to touch on all the intelligences:

- *Logical/mathematical:* she can produce figures showing demand for safe housing and a detailed account of the cost.

- *Visual/spatial:* she can show them a model of the new project or use graphs to display the demand information. She can even show them the architect's drawings.

- *Physical/kinesthetic:* she can take them to the proposed site and let them wander around while she describes where things will be. If the board or funders agree to the project, she can have a groundbreaking ceremony or symbolic bricklaying that the board is involved in.

- *Creative/musical:* she can play a recording of poems or songs written by women and their children who have been in the existing refuge. These songs reflect how important the refuge has been to them.

- *Emotional/interpersonal:* she can bring some of the women who've benefited from the existing refuge to talk about how the organization has changed their lives.

- *Intrapersonal:* she can appeal to the listeners' values, to their religious beliefs, to the mission of the organization (or the funder's organization). She can ask them to reflect on the stories of the women.

How Intelligent Are You?

Reflect on the intelligences. Can you think of colleagues or people in the public eye who have these intelligences? If you can, you might like to study them and how they react to different situations. In what kinds of situations are they successful and unsuccessful? How can you model their behaviors? To aid you in your thinking, you can make a chart like the one shown in Table 5.1 on page 108.

You may be starting to see there are a number of ways you can use the intelligences in breakthrough, and we'll be talking about this more. Right now we hope you agree that (1) you have all the intelligences to some extent; (2) you have some that are stronger, and you prefer to use those; and (3) there are others you need to work at or in which you perhaps feel you can't achieve.

Make a chart like the one shown in Table 5.2 and rate yourself

Table 5.1   From Whom Can I Learn?

Intelligence	Person	What Can I Learn?
Physical/kinesthetic	_____	_____
Logical/mathematical	_____	_____
Spatial/visual	_____	_____
Linguistic	_____	_____
Creative/musical	_____	_____
Emotional/interpersonal	_____	_____
Intrapersonal	_____	_____

on each of the intelligences. Use this rating scale: 1 = not so good and 10 = genius level.

Now think about which intelligences you'd really like to develop. You might want to do this for reasons other than organizational breakthrough—perhaps because they're interesting in themselves or because they would help you in your personal life. If you developed creative/musical intelligence, would it allow you to enjoy music more and use it as a stepping-stone to a rich inner world of imagination? Would it allow you to develop a stress-reducing hobby? What are the negative consequences of your not being as good as you could be in one or more of the various intelligences? To help organize your thoughts, use a three-column chart with these headings: Intelligence I Need to Work On, How Not Having It (or Enough of It) Reduces My Effectiveness, and How I Can Improve My Use of It.

Using the Intelligences to Sell Ideas

You can use your understanding of multiple intelligences to help achieve breakthrough in your organization.

• You might find, for example, that you've been trying to achieve a breakthrough using an inappropriate intelligence. Suppose

Table 5.2 Rating Your Intelligences

Intelligence	Score
Physical/kinesthetic	
Logical/mathematical	
Spatial/visual	
Linguistic	
Creative/musical	
Emotional/interpersonal	
Intrapersonal	

you had been trying to understand what it feels like to be a refugee by using a mathematical/logical approach, thinking "Well, my tent would be a quarter of the size of my house" or "I'd stand a 200 percent greater chance of catching an infection." Probably you'll find out more about the refugee experience by using your emotional intelligence or even the physical/kinesthetic aspect of the refugee experience. Put yourself in a camp, either in reality or in your mind. *Feel* what it's like. Make yourself a meal that would be eaten by a refugee. Try how it tastes. The British Red Cross (BRC), for example, gained a great deal of good publicity in a campaign about refugees by sending journalists a box of the basic camp survival kit. Many of the journalists wrote about the kit's contents, and the work of the BRC was treated sympathetically.

• As you read in "The Multi-Intelligence Breakthrough," you can use the intelligences to help sell your ideas to others or make your goals concrete for other people who have different intelligences. So, for example, describing how fabulous the architecture of the new theatre will be could work with someone who has strong visual intelligence. But that approach wouldn't work as powerfully with someone who has strong intrapersonal intelligence and needs to reflect on the purpose of the new venue and how it relates to the organization's mission.

• By creating a workplace environment that consciously

stimulates different intelligences, you can switch on the intelligences of your colleagues in the cause of breakthrough. (See Chapter Eleven for information on how to do this.)

The latter two points show the importance of intelligences as tools in *influencing*—making sure that your message gets through equally effectively to people whose intelligence preferences are different from yours.

Let's say you have a strong preference for the logical/mathematical intelligence. Your instinctive approach might be to say, "We should do this for the following [logical] reasons, and here are [the highly rational] advantages and disadvantages." Now if the person you are addressing works with a predominantly musical intelligence, she might not find your explanation convincing, particularly if her logical/mathematical intelligence is not developed. For this person you might want to use the metaphor of music to translate your idea into an appropriate format: "We need to get the rhythm right on this. Otherwise we're going to keep hitting bum notes."

Similarly, someone with strong intrapersonal intelligence needs more time to think about ideas and proposals. Pushing such a person for a quick answer to a query would be very uncomfortable for him. You're more likely to get an awkward silence than any cogent response. When working with someone like this, it's best to give him time and space to reflect.

Summary

Unlocking creativity is not easy, but it *is* easier if you're systematic about it. Here are some central ideas:

- Your brain has incredible potential, which you need to use to achieve real breakthrough results.
- By understanding how your brain works in terms of its *hardware* (neurological structure), you can help identify where you need to process information.

- By understanding some of the *software* the brain runs—the intelligences—you can improve your own ability to identify breakthroughs *and* encourage others to make them.

- Use of the various intelligences will also allow you to be more effective.

Action

You can probably improve access to your left brain and tighten up your logical thinking. If you're looking for kaizen breakthrough, that's the way to go. But to get into horshin breakthrough, you need to

- Come up with ways to stimulate your right brain quickly to solve challenges.

- Use your right brain, too, to gain commitment to your horshin goals: try stimulating it with some of the exercises we've suggested.

- Try to stimulate other people's right brains and tap into their intelligence preferences to gain commitment to the breakthrough.

- Make your workplace an environment that switches on all the intelligences.

Chapter Six

Creating a Smart Organization

How to Help Your Organization Learn

The gap between what an organization *knows* and what it *does* is a worrying phenomenon in many contemporary organizations.

> Why do organizations, or individuals who work in them, choose options that seem, in retrospect, obviously doomed?
>
> Why are policies put forward that have clearly failed before, only to be repeated again?
>
> Why do organizations fail to build on their learning or even share it properly?

In short, why do smart organizations do stupid things? Part of the answer is that organizations, and the individuals who work in them, sometimes seem reluctant to learn from experience or to develop what we call organizational wisdom or learning. (Nonprofits may, in some ways, be more prone to this phenomenon than are for-profit organizations, as the rather wry example in the passage about dead horses illustrates.) Our contention is that many organizations fail to make breakthroughs not because they're not creative or innovative but because they haven't learned to learn, and that to make *sustained* breakthroughs you have to become a learning organization. We go on to explore the idea of distinguishing knowledge and information and finally to some creative ways of managing knowledge.

We received an e-mail message about ways of dealing with dead horses and we adapted the suggestions to suit nonprofit organizations.

Nonprofit Strategies for Dead Horses

Dakota tribal wisdom says that when you are riding a dead horse, the best strategy is to dismount. This may seem obvious, but some larger nonprofits are reluctant to adopt this wisdom when it comes to the situations in which they find themselves. In our experience, many organizations would do *anything* to avoid even admitting the horse is dead.

The following is a list of strategies that nonprofits might come up with in their attempt to deal with the situation.

- Buy a stronger whip in the hope of improving performance.
- Change riders to get a better match of styles.
- Declare as a core value "The riding of horses is important in principle; their life status is not relevant."
- Appoint consultants or an action team to study the dead horse and come up with creative uses for it.
- Arrange to visit other nonprofits or, better still, private sector organizations to see how *they* ride dead horses.
- Rewrite the staff performance standards to incorporate riding dead horses as a core competence.
- Create a training program to help people ride dead horses.
- Alter the staff handbook to outlaw the use of the phrase *dead horse* as oppressive and judgmental.
- Form a quality circle or create a business process re-engineering initiative to find uses for dead horses.
- Promote the dead horse to a management position or create a special project role for it.

What Is a Learning Organization, and How Can It Help Promote Breakthrough?

The idea of the learning organization was developed and popularized by management guru Peter Senge in his book *The Fifth Disci-*

pline: The Art and Practice of the Learning Organization (1990). In this book, Senge took the concept of systems thinking and showed how it could be applied to organizations as learning organisms, so as to stop them from being trapped in a cycle of endlessly repeated mistakes.

Senge expanded his ideas in a second book: *The Fifth Discipline Fieldbook: Strategies and Tools for Building a Learning Organization* (1994). Both this and his earlier book are excellent introductions to the idea of learning in organizations.

It's perhaps worth specifying exactly what is a learning organization:

> *Learning in organizations means the continuous testing of experience, and the transformation of that experience into knowledge—accessible to the whole organization, and relevant to its core purpose.*

> —Peter Senge (1994, p. 49)

Senge's work is relevant to the whole of learning, but there are some key messages for those of us specifically concerned with trying to help our organizations achieve breakthrough:

- Continuously test experience: check out if what was true yesterday is true today. If it is, you can probably use kaizen to achieve breakthrough. If not, you need to work on horshin. (For instance, such organizations as Plan International and ActionAid might want to consider whether child sponsorship is still a good tactic for development.)
- Take experience and make it into a body of knowledge or *wisdom* that everyone can learn from. It's good that you had that one good idea. Now, how can you become systematic about disseminating it throughout the organization? (For example, could you mine your database to tell you how many donors could be transformationally upgraded in gift size to match those twenty big gifts that came in last year?)

- Make sure that learning is not simply academic or interesting but central to what you're about. This idea parallels the creativity-innovation split. It's not enough just to have good ideas. (You may have an interesting management development program in your organization, but to what extent does it really improve your service delivery?)

Are You in a Learning Organization?

You can judge your organization's learning processes by going through this checklist based on Senge's ideas:

- *Do you continuously test your experiences?* Are you willing to examine and challenge your sacred cows—not just during crises but in good times? What kinds of structures have you designed for this testing? When people raise potentially negative information, do you shoot the messenger?
- *Are you producing knowledge?* Knowledge, in this case, is information that creates the potential for effective action. Does your organization use information to create capabilities and competencies it didn't previously have? Do you feel that what you know is qualitatively different from the information you took in—is it "value-added"? (Distinguish, too, between data—simple facts and figures—and what these data *mean*.)
- *Is the knowledge and information shared and actively disseminated?* Is it accessible to everyone in the organization, from members of the board to front liners? Or are people walking around saying, "You know, I could have sworn we put out a report on this subject two years ago"? As a nonprofit, do you share information with other agencies in the sector?
- *Is the learning purposeful and relevant?* We need to be careful not to use the label *irrelevant* to screen out new ideas prematurely. New ideas are the basis of much experimentation and inspiration. But you can ask yourself, "Is this learning aimed at our core purpose? Can people make use of it?"

For example, the United Nations High Commission for Refugees (UNHCR) in Italy is wonderful. It raises ten times as much money from private donors as any other UNHCR branch in the world. In fact, it raises more money from individuals in Italy than the governments of Ireland or Belgium give to their national branches.

This extraordinary success is led by Lionello Boscardi and his small team of two, Alessandra and Federico. Lionello is good, but he's so busy that until recently he never had time to make detailed plans or to capture his techniques for others. His desk was littered with papers and books.

We spent almost a year with Lionello and his team, ostensibly writing a business plan. Actually what we were doing was attempting to determine (1) why UNHCR Italy is so much better than the others at fundraising from individuals and (2) which learning is unique to Italy—or to Lionello's team—and which could be transferred to other UNHCRs.

The result is a collection of organizational learning now being shared throughout the UNHCR family. (You might like to know, too, that in Italy they've set themselves a horshin goal to treble their income in three years.)

The Learning Cycle

It's important to understand *how* you learn if you're going to make the most of *what* you learn. David Kolb (1984), the educational psychologist, concludes that complete or rounded learning takes place when we complete a four-stage cycle, as illustrated in Figure 6.1.

Let's go through the cycle using a skiing analogy. A great deal of learning begins by doing something. We start skiing by getting out on to the bunny slope (action). We have a go at it. By the end of the day, we've discovered the vagaries of T-bar lifts, the secret of which way to lean as we ski, and how to transfer our weight to turn.

To "set" the learning, we need to take time in the evening to think about what went well and what less well (reflection). Better

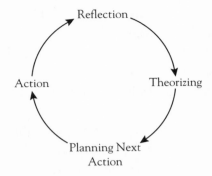

Figure 6.1   The Learning Cycle

Source: This representation builds on both Kolb's (1984) work and Charles Handy's idea of the learning wheel in his book *The Age of Unreason* (1990).

still, we might watch a video of ourselves. We build up a profile of what really happened. This, in turn, should allow us to start to formulate some theories, models, or general principles (theorizing) related to the subject of successful skiing. For example, if we learn to ski down an easy slope, we can take from that enough principles to ski down a steeper run. This theorizing then allows us to plan, practically, how to deal with situations and conditions well beyond our original learning environment (planning and next action). So we find ourselves on an exceptionally difficult run with lots of moguls. Although we might not know much about moguls, we can think back to what we learned about leaning and turning and use that to get to the bottom safely.

Sometimes the challenge is, of course, that we don't complete all the cycle. For example, we may spend too long in thinking and planning and reflecting—but not taking action. (This is what is meant by *paralysis by analysis*.) Eventually a breakthrough requires action!

Perhaps we become obsessed with *doing* and never spend long enough reflecting on what we have done, rendering us unable to identify the flaws in our practice, which in turn prevents our making the breakthrough. We keep trying to do the wrong thing better.

We may get stuck into a theory—some big idea—and not notice that it doesn't actually work. You could argue, for example, that the social and economic system that was communism was a big idea espoused by Karl Marx that simply didn't work. The bad news is it took almost ninety years for this to be demonstrated.

The Learning Individual

In his thirty years of research, Kolb established that we all have different preferences for one or more aspects of the learning cycle. (These preferences are another bit of variable brain software like the intelligences.) He categorized people and their preferences into four groups corresponding to the four parts of the learning cycle:

1. *Activists* prefer to learn by doing and hate sit-down, "talked-at," or reflective learning.
2. *Reflectors* prefer to learn by watching and observing, and dislike being thrust into the limelight or being pushed into hasty action.
3. *Theorists* prefer to build big pictures of things and draw out principles, and hate quick fixes and shallow explorations.
4. *Pragmatists* prefer to find out what works and are interested in what's practical, rather than to work on big theories or have lots of background knowledge.

Everyone can, of course, be all four to some degree, unless he or she is seriously dysfunctional. But, as always, we have preferences. Organizations and professions can also display distinct preferences. For example, because of the nature of their work, emergency relief agencies tend to be very action-oriented. Professional counseling operates much more through reflection and theorizing.

You may at some time hear people in your organization say one of these phrases:

"Let's just have a go at it."

"Can I go away and have a think about it?"

"What's the general principle here?"

"Forget about all the theory, what will we do?"

These kinds of statements usually indicate a person's learning style preference. As we've said, to access properly rounded learning you need to use all the styles, which probably means that you'll have to work on those styles with which you're less comfortable. List yourself and your immediate colleagues, organizing the names according to preferred learning style(s). You'll probably find that each person fits more than one category, but observe whether your team has an over-all preference, and then think about how all of you might access other styles. The following list gives you some hints on how to do that.

Current Learning Style	*How to Access Other Styles*
Activist	Pause before you act.
	Take time to draw up lists of positive and negative outcomes.
	Try to observe others and their actions.
Reflector	Have a go, take risks.
	Try to avoid observing others—let them observe you.
	Say the first thing that comes into your head.
Theorist	Try to look for quick-and-dirty shortcuts.
	Don't ask too many questions about "How risky . . . ?"
	Try to draw conclusions more quickly.
Pragmatist	Take longer to try to understand *how* things work.
	Read more books on topics—and choose hard books.
	Ask more Why? questions.

Breakthroughs and Learning Styles

Again, to be effective in a breakthrough you need to be aware of your own learning style and that of others, able to switch styles easily to maximize learning, and flexible enough to work in others' styles to help them learn.

The breakthrough, remember, could come out of any point in the learning cycle. Here are some examples:

- *Activist breakthrough:* Bob Geldof was so moved by the news reports from Ethiopia of the famine that he was galvanized into recruiting a whole gang of his show business friends to record a pop record to raise funds—"Do They Know It's Christmas?" From idea to released records, it took just two weeks to accomplish. Not content to stop there, Geldof went on to produce the summer event Live Aid in 1985. There was no grand plan to begin with. It just gained momentum.

- *Reflector breakthrough:* Colin McKenzie of the National Gallery in London (see Chapter Four) made his fifteen-foot breakthrough by reflecting. He studied what people did and then made his move.

- *Theorist breakthrough:* the games that Doctors Without Borders created (discussed later in this chapter) were the product of theorizing—from an organization naturally committed to *action* and *pragmatism*.

- *Pragmatist breakthrough:* Lionello Boscardi of UNHCR Italy is a great pragmatist; he's interested in what works—and for this reason it was a lot harder for him to work out some wider principles behind his success (*reflection* and *theory*) so that others could replicate it.

The Team and Organization Learning Cycle

Senge (1994) adapted Kolb's learning cycle for individuals as a tool to explore the idea that a team or organization can also go through it. We've taken it a step further, and the organizational learning cycle is illustrated in Figure 6.2.

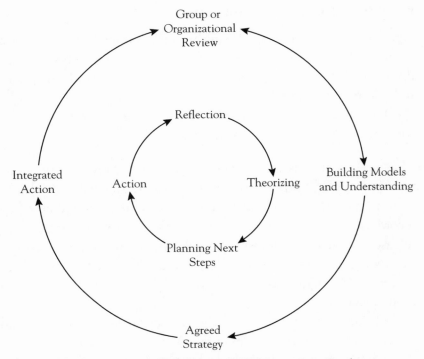

Figure 6.2   The Organizational Learning Cycle

Source: This representation builds on both Kolb's (1984) work and Charles Handy's idea of the learning wheel in his book *The Age of Unreason* (1990).

We can link organizational learning to breakthrough very directly. Let's assume you've identified that the breakthrough for your team is to launch a radical new service. In order to create real learning, you'll have to create opportunities at each stage of the cycle to help the team both understand and improve the service.

1.   *Group review:* Have you fully reviewed the past service? Do people understand its strengths and weaknesses? Will there be shared opportunities to review what happened once you've launched the service? Is there real reflection on the risks and opportunities of the new service? When will you review the service?

2.   *Building models and understanding:* How are the general principles of the service communicated? Do the general principles link to the vision, mission, and values of the organization? Is there a published plan that team members can refer to? Is there a plan for evaluation with success factors?

3.   *Agreed Strategy:* Do people plan together based on the complete cycle? How do people at the "bottom" of the organization have their ideas and input valued? Once you've completed phase one of the project, will people be able to feed in their ideas? Is it clear how targets have been set?

4.   *Integrated action:* Does everyone know what he or she has to do? Are people clear about what others have to do? Do they understand why you've made the change?

A breakthrough organization will work on the team stages of this process as well as on the individual learning elements. Of course, you don't just go round the cycle once. Having tried the new service, you need to go back into review, then build or extend the model you share and plan a revised strategy. After that you can develop some new integrated action. A willingness and ability to go round this cycle is vital to any organization keen to learn from its past and to make breakthroughs.

The cycle is a useful tool. It gives us the means to become a learning organization. But you can use the tool and still not succeed with the learning if what you're learning isn't knowledge.

Distinguish Knowledge from Information

Part of being a learning organization is having the ability to distinguish between knowledge and information or data. Often board members, managers, staff, and volunteers have lots of *information*, but they don't know what to do with it or what it really means.

Knowledge, in contrast, tells us *how* we're doing or guides us in what to do. A simple example that sums up the difference between knowledge and information is the experience we have on airplanes.

The staff give us lots of information: "Welcome aboard this Boeing 737. We're flying at thirty-seven thousand feet at a speed of 650 miles per hour. The temperature outside is −76°F." Lots of information—but how can we use it? Presumably they've told us we're flying at that height in that temperature so that we remember to wrap up warmly and hold on tight if we choose to go for a walk along the wing in midflight. . . . Lots of information—but what does it *mean?* Knowledge has meaning and a purpose. It's probably useful to hear, "The journey's going to take about seven-and-a-half hours. We're flying high to avoid air pockets. The evening meal—with three choices including vegetarian—will be served in about forty-five minutes." That's *knowledge.*

So a nonprofit may know what its financial results are. But what do those tell you about

- Whether the organization's money has been wisely or poorly used over the last year
- What the situation is now and whether this is a good or bad position
- What trends in the current data are finite and what are going to continue

We can only make breakthroughs using knowledge. And organizations need to be clear about what they *know* and what they *don't know.* Linked questions are *Who* should know? and *What can those people do* with this knowledge? These distinctions need to be managed while going round the organizational learning cycle.

Merlin and Doctors Without Borders Play Games with Knowledge

For the past three years, =mc has been running a weeklong program for the emergency relief agencies Médecins Sans Frontières (Doctors Without Borders) and its U.K. sister organization, Merlin. The program is built around the learning cycle. However, because the people who work for the organizations are strong activists, the program particularly emphasizes building models and understanding as a way of capturing and sharing knowledge.

As part of that program, we run a very challenging exercise. On day one the teams are asked to play with board games to see how they work. They are then given the task of constructing their own games over the next three days. They aren't given the whole time to do it— just odd slots of one to one-and-a-half hours between more formal sessions of management learning. So they're under pressure.

The games are constructed around explicit principles:

- Each game is on a given topic, including ones like these:

   "Vaccine": To whom should we give the vaccine if we have enough for only 50 percent of the village?

   "Stay-or-Go": The rebel troops are approaching—should we, the relief workers, leave, or should we stay with the refugees?

   "On Board": How do we persuade the local tribal chiefs to sanction men working with women when it offends local customs?

- Each game must be capable of being played by another team that knows nothing about the topic and must include a full set of rules.
- The game must simulate how decisions are reached and "real-world" accidents (a bit like Chance cards in Monopoly). The team playing it must report back that its *knowledge* of how to deal with the situation described has improved.

Participants in these courses usually begin by hating this part of the program. Inventing a game can seem like merely a roundabout way to gain how-to information on what to do in certain situations. Over the period of the program, however, the participants come to realize that the games are powerful ways to capture existing knowledge and to hypothesize about how to deal with nonstandard situations.

The Doctors Without Borders example touches on another important distinction: there is a difference between *tacit* and *explicit* knowledge. Most organizations have explicit knowledge systems in place, in the form of organizational diagrams, job descriptions, employee appraisals, and the like. But key knowledge may be *tacit*—that is, it may be inside someone's head or held by a particular group.

We need to work to get that tacit knowledge out. It often embodies some key general principles that underlie more specific, explicit knowledge. For example, the U.S. Marines undoubtedly study Clausewitz and Basil Liddell Hart, both great military strategists. But, according to John O'Keefe (1998, p. 84), "the marines rely mostly on three key bits of tacit knowledge: (1) keep on the move, (2) use surprise, and (3) take the high ground." As O'Keefe points out, these are, in general, excellent bits of tacit knowledge that need to be made explicit.

It's fantastically useful to be able to make your key knowledge explicit. A relief agency, for example, could perhaps sum up their "tactics" this way: (1) get there within twenty-four hours, (2) prioritize establishing clean water and shelter, and (3) keep families together. For an orchestra keen to build a broad customer base, the tacit knowledge to make explicit could be (1) mix "pops" with "challenges," (2) explain the challenges, (3) give people incentives to try the new.

Think about your own organization. What would you say was your explicit and tacit knowledge? Where is each kind kept, and by whom? How accessible is it? How can it be made more accessible?

Celebrate Failure

You may want to reread that heading. It says to *celebrate* failure. Not tolerate or accept or be reasonably understanding about, but *celebrate*. We say this because an important finding from our work with incredibly successful organizations is that a key condition of their success is the tendency not just to be risk-friendly but to actively *seek* risks. And if you're going to seek risks, you also have to learn to welcome failure as your most important and enriching learning opportunity. This links strongly to the integrated action part of the learning cycle. To succeed in breakthrough, you have to take risky action that has the potential for high payoff. But payoff is not guaranteed. This section looks at how you need to reflect on and then learn from this risky action.

Now we can hear some of you saying, "Ho hum, knew about the importance of failure ages ago," and you're right. For many commercial organizations it was a buzz phrase ten years ago. We have three questions for you:

Did you ever truly celebrate failure, or did you simply chant the mantra?

Is celebrating failure really a part of your culture?

Have you learned how to learn from the failure so you can plan successful next steps?

Often organizations *say* they celebrate risk taking, but their culture clearly works against this.

Before going any further, we had better draw a distinction between two concepts that are often inappropriately linked together. The first is *failure:* a genuine attempt to achieve a goal with maximum effort and energy. The second is *poor performance:* an ill-prepared or poorly executed piece of effort to achieve a goal.

Welcoming or rewarding poor performance is clearly a no-no. You don't want to create a culture in which failure to deliver becomes the norm. All that leads to is a low-achieving—or even nonachieving—organization. Sadly, many nonprofits don't deal strongly enough with poor performance. (See the passage "Nonprofit Strategies for Dead Horses" at the beginning of this chapter.) They may even avoid labeling it *poor.* There are many reasons for doing so: to avoid conflict, to be seen to be inclusive, to try to build people up, to avoid discriminating against various groups. But the reality is that poor performance is *poor.*

The poor performance itself can result from a range of causes, from poorly designed strategies to poorly executed activities. It's important that the nonprofit sort out and diagnose the challenge and resolve it. Poor performance will kill any breakthrough initiative before it's started. But that's the subject of a different book.

So what does it mean to *celebrate* failure? It means creating a culture or atmosphere in which people are encouraged to take appropriate and calculated risks. If they do fail, they and the organization have a systematic way to analyze and learn from the failure. (We're back to the idea of a learning organization.)

The Prince's Youth Business Trust Celebrates Failure

The Prince's Youth Business Trust (PYBT) is a U.K.-based nonprofit that works to help young people at risk enter the world of work by setting up their own businesses. It was established by Prince Charles and gets most of its money through corporate support. These companies see this work as part of their community investment. All the companies who contribute are themselves successful. As you would imagine, they are demanding donors who expect results.

A few years ago, we were working with a senior marketing executive at PYBT. He was nervous about a major donor presentation when he'd have to report to the business supporters about PYBT's achievements over the last year. He was nervous because he felt the charity was trapped in the "success graph," which looked something like the one in Figure 6.3.

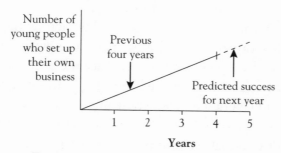

Figure 6.3   Predicted Success Graph

The marketing executive saw a problem: he knew that to produce this graph of past, present, and continued future success, the charity would have to do a number of things:

- Define "success" in more general—vaguer—terms. (We're back to dead horses.)
- Consciously select young people for grants who are really likely to succeed, and take fewer risks on young people on the margins of society.
- Present statistics and choose reporting time frames carefully so as to put the most positive spin possible on the results.

The executive's concern was not that he was lying but that he was managing the information to create an unstintingly positive impression that wasn't really in accord with the purpose of the organization's work.

We discussed with him whether this approach really matched the organization's mission, and we persuaded him to take what seemed like a big risk. We asked him to produce a new graph for the meeting with the major corporate donors. That graph looked like Figure 6.4.

What *this* graph showed was that the executive wanted the business supporters to sanction a *drop* in results for the next year. He wanted them to sanction a level of failure. That drop would actually represent an attempt by PYBT to take risk.

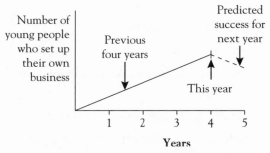

Figure 6.4   Proposed Failure Graph

He showed the graph at the meeting. There was a gasp and then a hush in the room as one hundred donors realized what he was proposing. Then the very brave marketing executive stood up and said, "Ladies and gentlemen, you all run your own successful businesses. You all know that 80 percent of new products fail. You all know that to really succeed you have to invest, take risks, ignore short-term gain for long-term results.

"I'd like you to back me in taking more risks, with 'riskier' young people, in order to achieve our mission. And that means our 'success' rate may go down. In fact, it probably will. By consciously identifying and helping young people less likely to succeed, we will probably lower the success line on the graph. But even the young people who don't manage to set up their own businesses will, I believe, still gain. And we will work hard to learn more about why young people fail."

After some silence, a few smiles passed across the faces of the audience. They got it. As their questions were answered they became clearer on what PYBT was trying to achieve and more aligned to the proposition. The results: donors who had a clearer understanding of the mission and its implications and who were more committed to it—and, you guessed it, an increase in funding.

To create a culture where risk—and its necessary corollary, failure—is truly celebrated, where you're much more likely to produce significant results, people must

- Be clear about their responsibilities.
- Have specific authority boundaries.
- Take responsibility for results.
- Be allowed to learn from their mistakes and be given the chance to correct them.
- Actively seek to learn from their misses and failures.
- Share the knowledge they gain with others in a public way.

Greenpeace International: The Dog's Bollocks

Greenpeace is perhaps the best-known international nonprofit working on environmental issues. Although part of a unified organization, each group works independently on many issues and is strongly committed to sharing experience.

Every year, Greenpeace International—the international alliance of all national Greenpeace organizations—brings all the member organizations together in Amsterdam. About five years ago, Daryl Upsall, then the international head of fundraising and marketing, introduced a contest called the Dog's Bollocks.

Essentially, it was a glitzy (at least by Greenpeace standards) Oscars-type ceremony during which each Greenpeace put forward its Greatest Failure of the Year—*and the learning they got from it*. Here are some contributions:

- One Greenpeace visited Russia and mistranslated a poster message. Instead of saying "Russia needs to deal with its rubbish," it read "Russia is rubbish." This group learned about the importance of linguistic nuance.

- Greenpeace in Australia messed up on a mailing. Instead of mailing the fundraising appeal to its supporters, the group sent out all the letters in the *return* envelope, thus mailing 200,000 letters to itself. This group learned the importance of introducing quality control and risk management before mailing.

Participants said the Dog's Bollocks was one of the most important parts of the international meeting because instead of boasting about successes—which they could do in the bar—they shared their calamities and from them gained real learning.

Summary

Many organizations suffer from a discrepancy, or gap, between what they know and what they do. This gap holds them back in a variety of ways.

Part of the solution is to become a learning organization. To find out if your organization *is* one, you should work through the checklist in this chapter (in the section "Are You in a Learning Organization?").

In addition, you need to think about the whole learning process at both an individual and an organizational level. Kolb's learning cycle can help you understand this. You also need to think about how you capture and disseminate *tacit* and *explicit* knowledge.

Action

- How does your organization capture learning? What's missing from the manuals and files? How could you better capture the knowledge your organization is holding?
- How do you celebrate failure (and not poor performance)? How could you do that better?
- What learning styles do you and your colleagues have and prefer to use? What actions can you take to strengthen and access those that are less well represented?

As a manager or board member, you have a special responsibility to help your colleagues and volunteers take and manage risks. There are two separate processes here: (1) encouraging people to take *appropriate* risks and (2) enabling them to manage the *level* of risk involved.

What is an appropriate risk will vary from situation to situation. For a very experienced operations manager in a developing country, an appropriate risk might involve challenging the government minister in a meeting about rural policy. The same situation could be too risky for a less experienced manager. Appropriateness can, of course, relate to the degree of risk for the organization. Committing all your funds to an unproven fundraising idea is probably taking an inappropriate risk. Look at what happened to many of the dot-com businesses.

Chapter Seven

Mapping the Possibilities

Organizing Your Thinking for the High-Payoff Idea

Earlier in this book we looked at why it's important to use new or different language—such as the terms *kaizen* and *horshin*—and new or different ways of communicating your breakthrough idea, such as through multiple intelligences. These approaches not only differentiate breakthrough thinking from "ordinary" thinking but also actively work to bring as many people as possible on board by appealing to the different preferences they have for taking in and processing data.

So we've seen that the communication for breakthrough needs to be different. But what about the actual *process* of organizing your thinking? This chapter introduces you to *mindmapping*®: a different way to organize and lay out your thinking. This way of working can in turn identify the breakthrough. The chapter also outlines how to create a mindmap, and it explores some different types of mindmaps and their uses.

What Is Mindmapping?

Most planning and thinking is done in a rational, sequential, left brain way. Mindmapping is a conscious attempt to get away from this sequential and vertical process, which tends to produce "regular" or "normal" results. Mindmapping also is an attempt to get away from the formats and materials that are associated with left brain thinking: 8.5″ × 11″ or legal-size paper, black letters on white paper, numbered elements, and so on.

Mindmapping is a visual and organic way of building a whole

connected and interconnected picture of a situation or issue in a single pass. It mirrors the complexity and messiness of real systems. It's also a way of relating the apparently unconnectable and can even be a way of disassociating ideas or actions that have always seemed to be intrinsic to each other. It's a technique to scope out or explore the possibilities, options, and developments implicit in an idea. It represents a radical way of using both halves of your brain to capture all the main ideas and messages in a given topic. It helps you change your thinking by changing format and style. In a mindmap, you use big sheets of nonstandard-size paper, hung landscape style, and colored pens. A mindmap won't necessarily *give* you a breakthrough idea. If you already have the idea, mindmapping will use both your left and right brain to help you produce a workable plan or scope out the issues you need to consider. If you don't have an idea, you will use both your left and right brain to prepare the ground—sometimes by thinking the unthinkable—from which the idea is most likely to come.

The concept of mindmapping was originally developed in the 1970s by Tony Buzan (1995), a British lecturer in adult education. He noticed that the adult learners he was working with often recalled, discussed, or planned things in interconnected bits or chunks, flitting from topic to topic, making links as they occurred. He also noticed that students often needed only one word or phrase or image to recall and explain a complex idea. He came up with mindmapping as a technique to model this nonlinear, organic thinking—seeing it as being a natural thought process that uses the whole brain. By displaying verbal information in a visual way, he argued, we gain the benefits of both right and left brain strengths— overview and patterns from the right, detail and specific words and data from the left. To share his idea, he originally wrote a book, *Use Your Head* (1995), and went on to make a popular TV series based on the book. Such has been mindmapping's global appeal that it has been used by organizations as diverse as Boeing in the United States (in its development and engineering of a new plane) and Amnesty International (in May 2002 to work out its radical, new, integrated strategic plan).

Figure 7.1 shows a mindmap for this chapter. You'll see that it contains the key information in the chapter, which is itself organized in more or less the usual linear way. But, as you can see, we gain advantages by laying it out in a graphic form: you can take it all in on one page, it shows you the *connections* between ideas and it focuses on overview rather than detail. Note that a mindmap doesn't *replace* the detail or narrative in writing. The mindmap will serve as a memory aid once you've read the chapter. It was also helpful to us as we outlined our ideas before writing the chapter.

Look again at the chapter mindmap in Figure 7.1, and you'll notice that we began with four major *branches:* Thinking and Organizing, Origins, How to Do It, and Advantages. (We could have added other branches—for instance, *disadvantages* or *uses*.) From each of these branches we created sub-branches. For example, coming out of Origins are two main branches: Buzan and Development. So a mindmap is *organized*—it does have *rules*. (This reminds us of the sonnet form in poetry; the *discipline* of the rules helps you be creative.)

The previous point about mindmaps not being strict replacements for text is important. Depending on what you are trying to do, mindmapping isn't always the best tool to use. By their very nature, building a bridge or rolling out a detailed service strategy are perhaps better suited to detailed and linear planning. Mindmaps are best for topics that are messy and "sticky" in the sense that bits connected at one point of the plan have an impact on and alter another point. Planning a community festival program, for example, is not usually a simple A to B to C process. "How many people" and "What kind of people?" are connected to "What kinds of activities?" and "What time of day?" are connected to "How big is the budget?"

Mindmapping looks easy, and it is *with practice*. Remember, though, that just as it probably took you a long time to get good at the linear approach to capturing and communicating thinking, you shouldn't expect this technique to "click" overnight. With practice, though, you'll find that mindmaps are actually quicker to generate and explain than conventional writing.

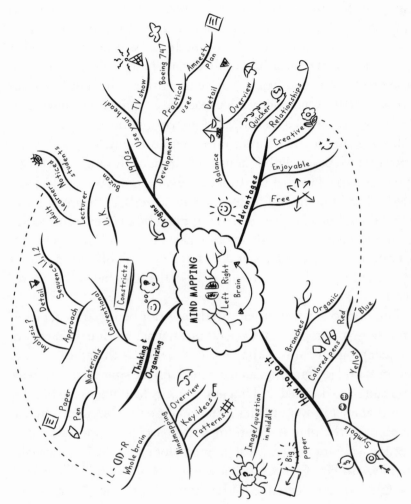

Figure 7.1   Mindmap for This Chapter

Creating a Mindmap

To create a mindmap you'll need the following items:

- A sheet of paper. Ideally this should be twelve by eighteen inches or bigger. Construction paper is perfect. (There's something about a piece of standard or legal size paper that makes you think of reports and other such official documents.) Use this paper on its side—landscape-style rather than portrait-style.
- Colored pens or pencils and some highlighters. Remember that color and visual information is processed on the right side of the brain. A black or blue pen is designed for left brain, rational thinking, so use as many colors as you can. Even try to use different sizes and types of pen.
- A surface to write on. A table is good, but think too about the floor or a wall as an alternative. Unusual surfaces, too, can make a difference in loosening up your approach.

Begin your map with a central graphic or phrase. And then create branches, followed by sub-branches. Remember, use:

- Key words or phrases—not sentences
- Graphics and symbols to complement words
- Images and patterns to make right brain connections
- Colors and shades to show priority and similarity
- Lines—dotted and normal to illustrate connections

Creating a Mindmap to Solve a Challenge

To take you through the process of creating a mindmap, we're going to use one to solve a hypothetical challenge. Suppose that you work for a school where there is a very high rate of absenteeism, and you are going to create a mindmap to explore how you might deal with this challenge.

Figure 7.2   Mindmapping, Step One

Before you even start, though, you discover that the way you choose to *phrase* the challenge has an impact on your approach: "How can we reduce absenteeism?" is quite different from "How can we help students love coming to school?" We suggest you use the latter wording because it

- Is positive
- Is *future*-oriented
- Uses a strong emotional verb, *love*
- Creates the mind-set for breakthrough

On to creating the mindmap!

Step One

Draw an image of the topic in the middle of the paper as well as a phrase or question. (Note that it's not important how good your drawings are—just that you have them.) Color it. Inside the shape you draw, write the focus of your thinking, ideally in the form of a question. For example, "How can we improve our income by 300 percent in two years?" or "How can we put women's interests at the heart of what we do?" The image and words are the *mission* of your mindmap. Figure 7.2 illustrates step one of the mindmap of our hypothetical school challenge. Notice how we've highlighted the word *love* and drawn a heart the way a teenager might.

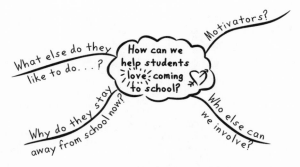

Figure 7.3   Mindmapping, Step Two

Step Two

Create some key branches off from your central picture. Use these branches as the main ideas that come to your mind when you think about this topic. They are the equivalent of chapter or section headings in a regular report. Don't be afraid to reinforce them with pictures. Make these branches look organic—that is, use curving lines that are slightly thicker near the center and thinner as they grow out. Write *on* each of these branches the phrase or key words that are represented by that branch.

As you look at Figure 7.3, notice that because these four branches are meant to be stimuli, they—like the first main stimulus—are also framed as questions. Also notice that the four branches are spaced such that you can add to them as other thoughts occur.

Step Three

Capture further key ideas by drawing lines radiating out from the four main branches. Draw one line for each key word or phrase. Print the words on the line to make them clear. Again, reinforce them with images or pictures. Don't be afraid to have lots of these. As mentioned in step two, make sure as you do this that you write *on* the line. If you write at the end of a line, you'll find that it stops or

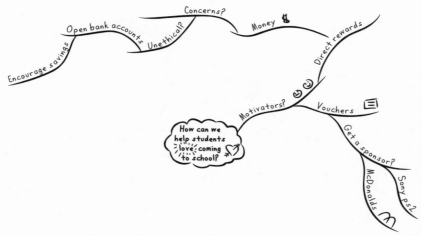

Figure 7.4   Mindmapping, Step Three

cuts off the flow. Also leave a little bit of line beyond where the words are. Doing so encourages "adding to."

Notice in Figure 7.4 that (1) the branch has gone off in a number of directions and (2) some things create Q&A links, others just generate lots of possibilities, and others run out of steam.

Step Four

Extend the existing lines by adding new ones to represent each new idea. You'll find that these main lines split into smaller sections, representing developments from the main idea. Again, use words, short phrases, or pictures and images. Typically you find you get down to detail here.

Looking at Figure 7.5, notice that

- There are connections among elements; for example, the idea of prizes and gifts comes up twice.
- There are some potentially good ideas and lots of terrible ideas.
- Some ideas need evaluation. For example, you could use a "smiley face" or "frowny face" symbol on *using DVDs as prize*.

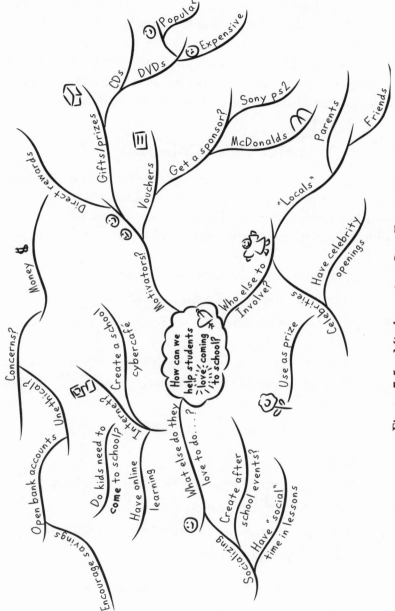

Figure 7.5 Mindmapping, Step Four

Step Five

Because this book shows only black and white, we can't demonstrate all of step five, which is when you reinforce the map with colors. The purpose of these is to help underline the key ideas and to stimulate the right side of the brain *at the same time* as the left. Link ideas with dotted lines. Use some colors to show linkages. Use highlighter colors to demonstrate similarities. Use other colors to show differences.

Other Uses of Mindmaps

In the example we've just worked through, we focused on mindmapping as a way of getting an overview and exploring relationships, as these are key for breakthrough. But mindmaps are not just for stimulating breakthrough. In our experience, there are three other main uses:

1. To capture ideas as you have them—*a dump*
2. To show an overview and relationships—*a map*
3. To record ideas and information—*a record*

Each of these uses requires slightly different approaches and emphasis. Here we've listed some tips on how to explore these other uses.

Using Mindmaps to Capture Ideas

- Go quickly.
- Do it for a short time, then come back to it again later.
- Stick to one color if that's easier.
- Don't worry about crossing out structures you've drawn.
- Use a really big piece of paper.

Using Mindmaps to Map Issues

- Go quickly through a first draft.
- Use lots of colors, and ideally if you have to circulate the mindmap, use a color copier.

- Be prepared to redraft.
- Work to make the structure clear.

Using Mindmaps to Record *a Meeting*

- Be clear about *what* you plan to record—actions, information, decisions, and so on.
- Make all the elements clear and readable.
- Use one color so that the record can be easily reproduced.
- Get the finished mindmap checked out by other people who were there.
- Use symbols and images that others will understand easily.

To find out more about these uses, read Tony Buzan's outstanding book *The Mind Map Book*, (1995).

Using Mindmaps in Designing Organizational Breakthroughs

We've used giant "group" mindmaps with a number of organizations. For example, we did one with UNHCR in Italy showing their vision and strategy for the organization. It was produced in a day at their headquarters in Rome. Capturing all the key ideas, it was then used as the basis for a subsequent strategic plan to submit to the international headquarters in Geneva. We used the same technique with a group of senior managers at the national agency, Victim Support Scotland, to map and solve a governance challenge.

These maps used the same principles we've talked about before except that they were done on a very large scale. This has the advantages of

- Making it more of a group activity
- Focusing the group's attention
- Allowing right brain stimulus

Mindmapping in a group also keys in to multiple intelligences: *kinesthetic* intelligence (you move elements around), *visual* intelligence (you can see the big—colored—picture), *interpersonal* intelligence (you do it as a group), and *intrapersonal* intelligence (you have a chance to look for patterns and significance). And if you play music while you work, you can also key into people's *creative/musical* intelligence.

Summary

Mindmapping isn't a substitute for other kinds of mapping, organizing, or planning; it's part of the toolbox. It *is* a useful technique when you want to think differently. Mindmapping

- Links to our natural thought processes
- Builds on right brain approaches
- Uses multiple intelligences
- Is quick
- Is enjoyable
- Can be done in a group or individually

To gain the most from it, you need to

- Practice
- Follow some rules
- Ask the right questions. For breakthrough you need to ask very good questions

You can use mindmaps

- As a giant "business plan" to put up in your reception area or main office
- As a single-page photocopy-reduced version given to each person

- As a stimulus to a wider debate
- As a tool to involve everyone in a collective exercise

Action

Try using mindmaps

- For your next business or strategic plan. Put up some large sheets of paper and create a mindmap that involves everyone.
- As a means of answering a good "How can we . . . ?" question in a group. It's worth brainstorming a list of questions to put in the center of the mindmap first.

Learning to do mindmapping effectively is a matter of practice. Begin with simple things. Try listening to the news and making a mindmap of what was said in real time. You'll be surprised at how easy it is. Then try this same technique for taking minutes in a meeting.

Chapter Eight

Balancing Creativity and Innovation

How You Can Get to the Breakthrough

A lot of this book has been about creativity. It's not enough, however, for a board, organization, unit, or team just to be *creative*. You also need to be *innovative* when going for breakthrough. But not every board, organization, unit, or team needs equal amounts of creativity and innovation at the same time.

This chapter explores how to *balance* creativity and innovation in your organization and how to maintain the innovation momentum—that is, the ability to continue to change and adapt positively.

The lesson from our experience is that many breakthroughs—even if they are apparently from out in left field—are often the result of simple hard work and simple rules applied consistently and methodically. A second lesson is that you need more than just techniques like suggestion boxes or quality circles; you need to create a culture and business structure that strongly reinforces innovation as well as creativity.

Meeting Need

The levels of creativity and innovation we want to experience as *consumers* vary depending on what product or service we're seeking. If you've just bought some software, you want it to be *creative* in the sense that it's up-to-date and incorporates the latest thinking and approaches. More than that, though, you want it to *work* or to be *innovative* in the sense that it's been tried and tested and will actually add to your productivity. There's nothing more frustrating than "buggy" software that doesn't quite do what it's meant to or crashes your system or incorporates some nice but not very well thought out idea. Think, for example, of the early versions of OSX for the Macintosh. We began writing this book using it. A breakthrough in OS design, it was called. Indeed it was very creative and different—but still buggy and the cause of major crashes until the software developers caught up. In retrospect, we'll stick with valuing innovation more highly when looking to meet our IT needs. Tried and tested versions cause fewer headaches.

In contrast, you go to see an experimental dance company for the creativity of its performance. You'll live with some imperfections in the staging, the costumes, or the set because the nature of experimental dance is that innovation—the ironing out of imperfections—is fundamentally less important. What you're looking for is excitement and challenge—and creativity.

If you go to a hospital for treatment, nine times out of ten you'd probably like the people there to say, "Yes, we know this illness. We've got a treatment that we've used for ages and that we know works. We can give you the latest refinement that has few side effects." You want that degree of innovation to make you feel safe and secure about something as important as your health. You would probably be reluctant to sign up for a radical new procedure that was untried and untested, unless you were desperate or the existing innovations simply didn't work.

Antibiotics are an example of something that was a radical breakthrough sixty years ago and that has now been adapted, refined, innovated, and improved many times over. Now, of course, "superbugs" have emerged that are no longer susceptible to antibiotics, so doctors and pharmaceutical firms are desperately looking for breakthrough with a whole new class of drugs.

The =mc Creativity-Innovation Matrix

A key challenge is to determine the correct mix of creativity and innovation for your organization. This mix may—and probably should—vary at different times, but you do need to consider what it should be at any given time and how your culture, management, and systems can sustain that mix.

Before we go further, let's again define what we mean by the two terms *creativity* and *innovation:*

> Creativity is the process of *coming up with ideas*—for new services for residents, for new fundraising techniques, for new approaches to customer care, and so on. The ideas can be brilliantly obvious and logical or "weird." They may well be, or seem to be, impractical.
>
> Innovation is the process of coming up with *practical applications for such ideas* or of choosing one or more creative ideas on the basis of their delivering useful and achievable results. Thus residents *value* the new service, the fundraising technique *works*, and the customers *feel more cared for*.

Clearly organizations need to mix creativity and innovation in different measures, in different circumstances. Often they'll also need different amounts of creativity and innovation at different stages in a project.

Jubilee 2000: Overnight Creativity and Innovation

Jubilee 2000 is the umbrella name for a worldwide network of non-profits that was set up to persuade the developed nations to cancel the debt owed to them by developing countries. =mc worked with the senior team of Jubilee 2000 and their imaginative and inspiring CEO Ann Pettifor to come up with creative suggestions on how to make an impact at the Okinawa Summit of the World Bank and G8 in July 2000.

We were under a lot of time pressure and had only three hours to find the publicity stunt that would capture world headlines. Together we created a mindmap exploring a whole range of ideas, much as we demonstrated in Chapter Seven.

The one idea we agreed was the best when we were all in London involved a lot of planning and implementation. When the seven members of Jubilee 2000 got to Japan, however, they discovered it simply wasn't practical. It seemed they didn't have a good stunt to capture those headlines after all.

As luck would have it, the Japanese government suggested that rather than a cancellation of Third World debt, what was really needed was a lessening of the digital divide through more aid to developing countries in the form of computers. Although an interesting idea, this scarcely met the concerns of Jubilee 2000 groups. The group at the conference, however, wondered how they might use this proposal to their advantage. The team went back into a *creative* session to generate lots of ideas. They then went into an *innovative* session to choose a publicity stunt that effectively addressed both the Japanese suggestion and the goals of Jubilee 2000. Overnight, they came up with the inspiration to burn a laptop on the beach to highlight the futility (and self-interest) of Japan's proposal. They then had to be creative about how to set a laptop on fire. (It's not easy.) Eventually they tried lighter fluid and discovered it made a great photogenic flame. This image was widely used on television and in the press to help Jubilee 2000 gain the publicity they were seeking.

This case demonstrates in a very simple and practical way how nonprofits need to be able to move nimbly (and sometimes very quickly!) between creativity and innovation so as to cope with changing circumstances.

=mc has developed a matrix that helps you *define your current approach* in terms of creativity and innovation and then identify *what your approach should be*. As illustrated in Figure 8.1, the matrix shows the nine possible relationships of three different amounts or degrees of creativity and innovation exhibited by an organization.

Using the Matrix

Step one: plot your organization on the matrix. Where do you think

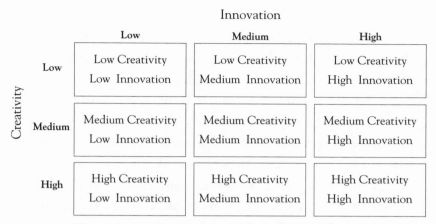

Figure 8.1   Creativity and Innovation Matrix

it is *now* in terms of creativity and innovation? You might want to consult colleagues or even neutral observers on this subject to gain a rounded perception. It can also be interesting to ask a number of people to do this step individually at a workshop and then compare answers to see how similar—or different—everyone's perceptions are. Part of sharing differences will be about sharing information or data on *why* people think the organization is in that position. It will be important, at that point, to agree on the common "measures" you're using to decide where the organization is. Once that's done, you're more likely to come to a consensus about which box the organization fits into. Then you can try to answer the questions listed in Exhibit 8.1 on page 152.

Step two: do the same exercise on your *key competitors*. Are they more or less creative, more or less innovative? Bearing in mind that you are making a subjective judgment, you should if possible try to apply the same criteria or measures you developed to establish your own position. (It's important not to fantasize about the competition) Make a list of your key competitors and then plot them on the matrix. You can then ask the same four questions listed in Exhibit 8.1.

Step three: decide whether or not your organization's position is

Why is the organization here? What are the factors that have positioned it here? Money, history, management, user need . . . ?

How did the organization come to be here? By choice, by accident, as a result of circumstances . . . ?

What are the *advantages* of this position? We work to our strengths, we're leading the field, it works for us . . . ?

What are the *disadvantages* of this position? We rely too much on other organizations' ideas, we're living off past glories, we can't keep up this pace . . . ?

Exhibit 8.1   How Did the Organization Arrive Here?

appropriate for its current goals or needs. This may require some analysis or reflection. At various phases in your organization's life cycle, for example, you may want to concentrate more on being creative or more on being innovative. Your need to be more creative or innovative may also depend simply on the nature of the business you are in. Are you a leading-edge, contemporary art gallery or a reference library?

Or, linking this activity directly to the subject of the book, you may want to decide how appropriate your current position is for breakthrough. What would you need to achieve breakthrough: more innovation or more creativity?

Matrix Analysis

Finally, it's time to decide if you want to change your position in the matrix. Figure 8.2 shows the same creativity-innovation matrix as in Figure 8.1, this time giving more detail as to the nature of the organization in each position. If you want to change, how would you do this? Let's look more closely at each of the boxes.

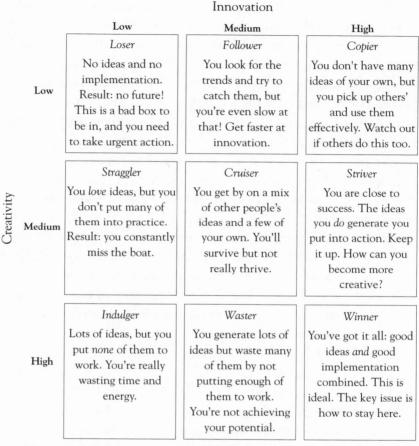

Figure 8.2   Summary of Organizational Types in Terms of Creativity and Innovation

Boxes 1 and 2: our experience suggests that any organization in either of these boxes is probably going to *fail* in the overall scheme of things. If your organization is in box 1, it's barely alive! We call it a *loser.* In box 2 you're a *straggler,* with not enough innovation to do anything serious with the good ideas you do have. Losers hardly ever make it out of the starting gate. Stragglers have potential, but they just can't seem to realize it. They need to acquire some techniques for identifying their good ideas and working through them systematically to pull out the ones to support and develop.

Box 3: in box 3 you're also in danger of failure despite incredible creativity. We call organizations in this box *indulgers*. (They throw away all their good ideas.) It's just not enough to be spectacularly creative—you've got to *implement*. Otherwise you run the significant danger of becoming internally focused to the exclusion of all else. A famous commercial example is the Beatles' ill-fated Apple Corporation. Artists were signed up and encouraged to experiment, but they rarely produced any saleable music. Endless parties and events predominated in the hope that these would engender a "creative" atmosphere. Maybe they did, but this approach led as well to fraud, the financial demise of the company, and lots of bad feeling over who was to blame.

In our experience, arts organizations are most likely to be guilty of falling into the indulger category. And the more they get criticized for indulgence, the more they tend to go into a "no one understands us" mantra. An ill-focused passion for "integrity to the cause" and lack of realism about customer needs can also lead to the failure to implement effectively.

Royal Opera Indulgence

For several years the Royal Opera House in London was a good example of an indulger. In many people's opinion, the company produced a range of performances that engaged and excited the staff and artists but not the audience. Elaborate sets were commissioned, designed, and then cast aside when the stage crew found they couldn't practicably change them given the time constraints of a performance. The productions were hugely over budget and extravagant. They opened late and weren't enthusiastically received. They were unsuccessful at the box office and among critics.

The reaction of artists and management within the organization was to complain that they needed more money and that the critical reaction meant the philistines were at the gates. They didn't recognize that many of the challenges were brought on by the company's own shortcomings. The result was a reputation for indulgence—a focus on unpurposeful creativity. Eventually the CEO and entire board were obliged to resign—guilty of mismanagement, according to a government investigation. After five CEOs in four years, it was only when a new, pragmatic regime took over that things looked up for the Royal Opera House.

Box 4: an organization here is likely to *get by*. It's not creative, but it does make some innovations, probably by taking the path that other organizations have trodden before it. It's a *follower*. It's unlikely to grow significantly using this strategy, and it needs to keep its eye on what others are doing to pick up on key trends. But it *can* succeed in a modest way. One challenge with this position is that lots of organizations are followers, looking for what works and pirating it. It's not unusual practice in the commercial sector. For nonprofits it may be legitimate to copy and model what's seen as good practice, but doing so doesn't give them an edge in terms of seeking funding or really cracking a key challenge.

Legacy Technique Adopted by Organization in Box 4

Legacy programs became a well-established way in the 1990s of securing planned gifts from major donors, thanks to some breakthrough work by Ken Burnett, founder of the influential Burnett Associates agency, who has written widely on the subjects of annual reports and relationship fundraising. The technique Burnett pioneered was simple: use an off-the-page advertisement or direct-mail letter to persuade donors to write in to your nonprofit for a free will-making pack. The pack helped donors write their own will at no or low cost and encouraged them to make a donation to whatever cause had supplied the pack. This strategy formed part of their long-term planning.

Relationship fundraising guru Ken Burnett developed the best and most original of these packs—a breakthrough in its time. It very cleverly didn't ask initially for a legacy but simply offered free will-making advice. His approach helped a number of charities make significant legacy acquisitions. But soon everyone wanted to use the same technique and even more or less the same pack. Everyone wanted to take advantage of an approach that seemed to work easily.

As a measure of how quickly this spread, within two years the U.K. Association of Legacy Administrators had grown from five to seventy-two members. Too many people—too many followers—wanted in on what quickly became a crowded market, and there wasn't enough space for them all to succeed. The result was a very rapid falloff in the effectiveness of this approach.

Box 5: an organization in this box will survive, but it won't ever really take off. It's average. It's a *cruiser*. It's therefore very vulnerable to being seen as the same as other organizations or at least no different in its goods or services. IBM stayed here for some years with its technology, then almost died as more progressive companies overtook it. The International Red Cross lost funds to new "aggressive" relief agencies like Doctors Without Borders in the 1990s because they stayed too average. Doctors Without Borders adopted aggressive and imaginative marketing techniques aimed at both individuals and governments. Cruiser organizations can feel comfortable because of the average results they get—"There are organizations worse than us . . ."

Box 6: an organization in this box is a *waster*. It has real potential. It has lots of creative ideas, yet doesn't have systematic approaches to implement them. The organization is likely to lose people (and ideas), and there may be a high degree of frustration. Your organization is probably a waster if you hear people saying, "It's all talk around here, and then nothing happens." This was the case in the mental health charity MIND. They were the people who first introduced the idea of sponsored adventure events—in this case parachute jumps. But they failed to capitalize on their first-move advantage. Other charities quickly saw the potential and made good, while MIND lost out.

Box 7: an organization in this box will, in the short term, sometimes do very well by copying or adapting other people's ideas—hence the name *copier*. But it needs to be aware that it can spend too long on innovating what is inevitably yesterday's idea. It needs to improve its creativity to really gain an edge. If your work is too focused on bor-rowing best practice from elsewhere, you may do well, but you won't excel. You're also vulnerable—to other people's ideas drying up and to other organizations implementing them better than you.

In the commercial world, Microsoft has been an exceptional box 7 organization: low, some would say, on creativity but able to pick up and run with others' ideas. For example, look at how the company adopted principles of the intuitive interface developed by Apple and Xerox and developed Windows. Indeed, Microsoft has done this to such an extent that it's no exaggeration to say the corporation has reached a position of world domination. However, even Microsoft has finally come to realize that relying on other people's ideas is not enough. In 2001 the company set up a department to *create* ideas as systematically as it is able to *innovate* them.

It's OK to Be Wrong; Just Change Your Mind and Get on with It

A good example of Microsoft's innovation orientation and, perhaps as important, its ability to get it wrong and then get it right, is its response to the Internet. At first Bill Gates thought the Internet was not going to be important. At a Microsoft conference in April 1995, he is rumored to have said,

An Internet browser is not a useful piece of software.

But he and the people at Microsoft soon changed their minds when they saw the potential of Netscape. By October 1995, only five months later, Microsoft had made a radical commitment to the Inter-net, buying up Internet companies and investing billions in research. Within a couple of years, Microsoft's own browser, Explorer, would be the market leader.

It's fine to get it wrong. You just have to be able to admit it and then catch up.

Box 8: this kind of organization will, in general, do well. It's a *striver*. It stays on top of its innovations and maximizes their potential. UNICEF was creative and innovative in its use of Christmas cards for many years. But then it was too slow to change when other nonprofits entered the market. In recent years, UNICEF has allowed its competitors to catch up. By not keeping ahead of the game, UNICEF and its Christmas cards have been relegated to box 5.

Box 9: this is the ideal situation: your creativity and innovation are in complete synchronization. You are systematic about both. You are a *winner*. Examples of such organizations are few and far between. 3M, with its public commitments to ensuring that 25 percent of its products are less than two years old, is a commercial example that comes to mind. In the nonprofit sector, there was certainly a time when Doctors Without Borders was at the leading edge of creativity and innovation in relief practice. So much so, indeed, that the Canadian management guru Henry Mintzberg studied the organization as part of his research. He followed the CEO around on the pillion of his motorbike for a week to see what he did. Through its creativity and innovation, Doctors Without Borders was able to implement a number of new ideas in organizing for relief. The organization was also creative and innovative in the way it approached publicity and PR.

Venture Philanthropy

Increasingly, at least in the United States, there's an acknowledgment that philanthropy has in the past tended to support the safer, more established causes and solutions (box 5 or 6).

A number of individuals and foundations have tried to break away from this tendency and take on the ideas of venture capital firms—that is, firms that consciously look for younger start-up concerns with high growth, high risk, *and* high return.

Exceptional in this work is Sterling Spurling, director of the Peninsula Foundation, an innovative foundation in San Mateo County, California. In 1999 he ran the Venture Philanthropy Roadshow. This involved taking a project bus around to a range of organizations actively seeking radical ideas to meet social need, and putting forward examples of exciting and challenging projects he had supported. In pursuit of the new and different, he even sponsored an =mc workshop on breakthrough thinking to help local nonprofits and service agencies come up with those ideas.

You might want, now, to think again about your creative and innovative position (and that of your competitors) and where you want to be. Before you head straight off for box 9, however, consider these points:

- Look back at what you said were the *advantages* and *disadvantages* of your current position and refine them, if necessary.
- Think about which competitors have the edge on you. *What* is their edge, and *why* do they have it?
- Ask yourself what box you *really* want to be in and what advantages and disadvantages it would have.

Next Move Case Study

Let's take the example of an imaginary charity that works with elders, Grey Action. Grey Action provides a range of social care services, mostly in the form of day care to people ages fifty-five to seventy. The organization currently positions itself in box 4 as a *follower*. It's arrived there over the past ten years by gradually building on ideas and good practice from other organizations.

There are *advantages* to this position:

- Grey Action's work is good and solid.
- It is well regarded among similarly traditional peers.
- Many funders like Grey Action's work because it's safe and uncontroversial.
- It is well able to meet the needs of its current key customers.

There are some *disadvantages* too:

- The organization is quite slow at adopting new ideas.
- It is losing some staff precisely because the work seems predictable and unoriginal.
- It's increasingly hard to gain funding for mainstream work because lots of other agencies are "following the follower."
- Grey Action's social care model doesn't meet the needs of all its customers, some of whom want more political campaigning on rights and pensions.

At a recent vision exercise, Grey Action management and staff came up with some challenges. One is that elders are living longer; in the next ten years many more will be in the eighty to ninety-plus age group. They're more likely to be "frail elderly" and will need very different skills and resources for their care than those that Grey Action currently provides.

Another challenge is that a number of Grey Action's ex-employees have joined other more politically "aware" organizations and are actively working to help them become leading edge in a way that never seemed possible at Grey Action. Other experienced and able staff are being poached by smaller agencies keen to follow Grey Action's model.

Grey Action is not in a good position. It needs to move, at least for a while, to box 8 or 7 to generate some new ideas and practice. (Notice that—in true breakthrough mode—they've chosen to look at the bigger challenge, box 8, before box 7.) The organization needs to decide what direction it wants to go.

To move into box 8, to become a *striver*, Grey Action would need to

- Create better internal systems to pick up on and nurture new practice

- Build in an incentive for staff to come up with new ideas, perhaps through a bonus or salary program

- Develop project teams and champions to see through good ideas

To move into box 7, to become a *copier*, Grey Action would need to

- Actively study best practice elsewhere

- Be quicker off the mark at adopting what's best

- Hire people from some of those rival organizations

- Ask consultant gerontologists to advise the organization on future trends

Grey Action has a choice and has to take some strategic action to back up that choice. What would your advice be?

Keeping Innovation Momentum: The Example of 3M

One challenge that often emerges from our work with organizations striving to become innovative is how to ensure that innovation is carried on as a continuous process and not simply as a brief response to some crisis or challenge.

The company usually regarded as one of the most creative and innovative in the world is 3M. Although 3M makes many prosaic products—adhesive tapes, abrasives, cleaners, films, and so on—it has managed to become extraordinarily creative and innovative about how it consistently comes up with new products and adapts existing products. It is very successful and very profitable. In our consulting and training work, we have often directed nonprofits, keen to improve their practice, toward 3M to study it.

The company has a well-documented approach to the creativity and innovation process, some of which we've included here because nonprofits can learn much from it. The interesting thing is that 3M's approach is not essentially complex or sophisticated. The company has established four key principles that it applies systematically and consistently:

1. Commit to experimentation.
2. Promote individual creativity.
3. Set breakthrough targets.
4. Integrate rewards and awards.

These principles, based as they are on almost 100 years of 3M experience, have some weight and authority. Central to 3M's success is the first principle, *commit to experimentation*. Above all, the people at 3M want products that work, but they recognize that to achieve this result, they have to be prepared to fail. One of 3M's earliest personnel manuals, dating from 1925, says,

> *Every idea evolved should have the chance to prove its worth, and this is true for two reasons: 1) if it is good, we want it; 2) if it is not good, we will have purchased our insurance and peace of mind when we have proved it impractical.*
>
> —*3M Technical Manual*, quoted in
> Kanter, Kao, and Wiersema, 1997, p. 54.

With regard to the second principle, *promote individual creativity*, Dr. William E. Coyne, senior vice-president of research and development at 3M, says, "Managers at 3M do perform such traditional tasks as clarifying the company's goals and setting objectives. We let our people know what we want them to accomplish. But—and it is a very big *but*—we do not tell them how to achieve those goals. We think by giving employees the freedom to find new paths to new solutions we are unleashing their creativity" (Coyne, 1997, p. 54). The first two principles are embodied by 3M's institutionalized innovation rule, which allows technical staff to spend up to 15 percent of their time on projects of their own choosing. Managers don't need to approve or even be told of the projects undertaken.

The Provenance of the 15 Percent Rule

During a lab visit in the early 1970s, William McKnight, then CEO of 3M, found a quality control specialist, Richard Drew, working on a strange "crinkly" tape. Drew explained that he'd noticed on a visit to a car body shop that spray painting two-tone cars was messy and unreliable. This process used one of 3M's existing tapes. When the tape was removed, it sometimes damaged the paintwork. Thus Drew was trying to invent a tape that was crinkly and therefore easier to remove from newly painted car bodies.

McKnight ordered Drew to give up the project, pointing out that Drew was in quality control—making tape for manufacturing was something he knew nothing about. And anyway, McKnight said, it was probably a stupid idea; the whole point of tape is for it to stick flat: 3M had spent years getting rid of the crinkles.

Drew ignored the order and went on developing the tape—a product we today call masking tape, which proved to be one of 3M's revolutionary products and is extensively used in the painting industry.

As a result of this experience, the chastened, and wiser, McKnight recognized that creativity is both hard to define and not the sole preserve of so-called creative people. Anyone, even someone in a traditionally analytical job like quality control, can be creative. (He also realized that it's impossible to *stop* creativity; it will find its way out.) He introduced the 15 percent "no management sign-off" rule specifically to encourage creative individual behavior and make it systematic (Coyne, 1997, pp. 46–48).

The third principle is *set breakthrough targets*. Until 1992, 3M had a target to achieve 25 percent of annual sales from products that had existed for a maximum of *five* years. In 1992, L. D. De Simone, the chairman and CEO of 3M, became aware that product cycles were shrinking, customer needs were changing more quickly, and technologies were accelerating, so he announced a new goal. It was unequivocal: 30 percent of all sales must come from products less than four years old. That goal, now being regularly achieved, was designed to model the market's need for products. It also led to more radical changes and stimulated the launch of a whole new spin-off company, Imation, to handle imaging and data management projects. (Imation may well have made the floppy disk or CD you use in your computer.)

The fourth key principle is to have an *integrated rewards and awards* system. Salary increases and promotions are, naturally, part of that deal. And if you come up with a winning product, you can receive a significant bonus. But 3M also has a number of other more general programs to stimulate innovation, including the following:

> *Technical Circle of Excellence:* this is a peer-voted status for which coworkers are nominated at a division or corporate level. The emphasis is on technical achievements' being recognized by colleagues. This status is awarded not only for personal achievement, but also for mentoring others to make such achievements.

> *Genesis grants:* if you come up with an idea that doesn't fit into your division's business plan, you can apply at the corporate level for a Genesis grant. These grants, for $15,000 to $75,000, are for innovative or leading-edge projects. They are primarily designed to help individuals cross-fertilize throughout the company.

> *Alpha grants:* these grants complement the Genesis grants. They are to encourage innovation in administrative and marketing areas. Alpha grants tend to be smaller and can be for ideas on how to improve filing or to reduce time spent in meetings. Anyone is eligible for these, and they help reduce the tendency to divide sales and marketing from research and development. They are also designed to demonstrate that creativity and innovation can come from anywhere in the company.

Amnesty International and Innovation

People think of Amnesty International (AI) as one organization. Actually it's a network of separate, country-based organizations working under a common charter. They also have an international secretariat that provides coordination and links. In recent years AI has set up an international innovation group specifically to look at fundraising. This group has members from all over the world, including the United States. Guided by an experienced facilitator, members meet two or three times a year to share their best and most radical ideas on fundraising. They then take these ideas back to their own national organizations to see how they can implement them.

One good example is the introduction of the fundraising technique known as direct dialogue. In direct dialogue, canvassers approach individuals in the street and ask them to become supporters of the organization by signing up for a subscription. This technique has been shown to work in places as far apart as Australia and Austria.

There was serious debate in the fundraising innovation group about whether this technique would work in countries like Sweden or the U.K., with a tradition of privacy. But it was adopted in those countries as well and now forms a significant part of AI's income.

Under its current director of international fundraising, Mark Hengstler, AI now hopes to refine and develop this approach further—trying to swap and share fundraising ideas across the globe and to become a genuine learning organization.

Applying the 3M Approach in a Nonprofit Setting

Unfortunately, we haven't found a nonprofit that has an approach as thought through as 3M's. True, Amnesty is doing some interesting work in fundraising, and Greenpeace not only shares campaigning techniques but also looks to create greener technologies to achieve its goals. Also AED in Brazil has exported a number of its learning technologies to Portugal and Mozambique. However, relatively few nonprofits have well-developed programs that might serve as models, so we think it's worth looking at how you might apply the 3M approach in your own organization. Table 8.1 on pages 168 and 169 lists some ideas and our suggestions for applying them in your work.

Although, as we said, nonprofits haven't worked out complete programs for systematizing creativity and innovation, they have come up with smaller-scale approaches that you might consider applying in your organization.

Set up an R&D department. The Academy for Education and Development (AED) in Washington, D.C. (not connected with the Brazilian NGO mentioned earlier), is a nonprofit that uses education to promote social change in the United States and overseas. Its work ranges from providing health education for teenage girls in a number of U.S. states to operating college-level leadership programs for nonprofit leaders in developing countries. AED set up a special unit—based on the idea of a commercial research and development function—specifically to nurture a culture of innovation within the organization.

Hire an artist. Another approach is to hire an individual to stimulate a new kind of culture. Many organizations turn to artists to fill this role. An artist or a poet in residence at a big commercial company is less unusual these days than it once was. Mishcon de Reya was Princess Diana's legal firm and one of the grandest and most stuffy legal firms in the United Kingdom. (They guided the princess during her divorce from Prince Charles.) Even it has had a poet in residence.

A number of prisons have also used artists to try to tackle issues of violence and rehabilitation. Two U.S. artists working in the United Kingdom, Ken Woolverton and Beth Shadder, brought with them ideas they had seen working in their own country about using creative arts to help deal with some of the most challenging prisoners. They visited one of the United Kingdom's most notorious prisons, Barlinnie, in Glasgow, Scotland, with a reputation for housing some of the most hardened criminals. They began by using murals as a way to help the prisoners change their environment. The work built from there to involve music, creative writing, sculpture, and even drama. An extraordinary bond grew between the artists and the prisoners, one that dramatically changed the culture and reduced violence and tension. The work at Barlinnie was inspirational for the inmates and for a number of people working in the criminal justice system. It has been widely copied.

Link up with a company. MENCAP, the U.K. charity that works to promote the interests of people with learning difficulties, won a national award in 2001 for a collaboration between it and British Gas, a leading gas provider. The way it worked was that every time a British Gas employee came up with a good idea to save money or innovate a product or service, the company paid MENCAP an agreed-on amount of money. Over a year, this amounted to a tidy sum. British Gas also agreed to pay a further sum for every production and repair team that went a month without having an accident.

There are many companies with a reputation for creativity and innovation—Virgin, Rubbermaid, and 3M to name just three. Try to link up with one to see how you could benefit and how you could exchange some of your approaches.

Laughter as a Way of Promoting Innovation and Creativity

We often think of India as a country with a long tradition of serious philosophical thought and meditation. And it is. But it's also the home of Laughter Club International, a nonprofit whose published mission is to bring "health and world peace through laughter."

The club, run by general practitioner Dr. Madan Kataria, was set up in 1995. It now has almost sixty thousand members in India and another ten thousand around the world. Kataria founded the club in Bombay (now called Mumbai) after observing how his patients' immune systems seemed to improve following laughter sessions. (This idea has some scientific backing. Laughter releases endorphins, the body's natural painkillers.)

Table 8.1 Applying the 3M Principles

Principle and Example	Key Questions for Nonprofits	How You Could Apply the Principle
Commit to Experimentation Greenpeace has a special innovation unit in Austria, which responded to the CFC gas concern by developing the technology to make refrigerators "greener." (Greenpeace then *gave the technology away* to the manufacturers to ensure its adoption.)	• Do you encourage experimentation at the headquarters, regional, or local level? • Do you give training in experimentation or creativity? • Is an explicit commitment to experimentation built into your values, beliefs, or mission? • Can you integrate this commitment to experimentation into the organization, or do you need to separate it?	• Set up a special task force that actively promotes experimentation. • Create challenge grants—up to $500 to try ideas in service areas or administration. • Move staff around to try different things; try job swaps among organizations.
Promote Individual Creativity The Gulbenkian Foundation had a program in the 1990s that allowed individuals to apply for grants to pursue radical ideas	• How does your nonprofit promote or encourage individual creativity? • Do you give your people enough freedom to experiment? Are they clear about the extent to which they can bend the rules? • Are creativity and innovation recognized in every department or section?	• Replace "dress down" day with "wild idea" day. • Devise a creativity award for each department. • Encourage people to express ideas in songs, paintings, collages, and the like rather than in reports.

Principle and Example	Key Questions for Nonprofits	How You Could Apply the Principle
Set Breakthrough Targets Begin with a vision. UNHCR in Italy began by saying, "Let's treble our budget in three years." The organization then worked back to say, "How could we achieve this?!"	• Are you committed to too many *incremental* targets? • Do you have measures for breakthrough or innovation? • Who sets the goals in your organization, and how are they set? • Do you distinguish between horshin and kaizen goals? • Do you set targets based on *potential* rather than on what you think is *probable?*	• Begin by asking, "What could we achieve if we had three times as much money?" Then think about how to do it rather than why it would be difficult. • Create a mission with stronger *action* words: *abolish, conquer, ensure,* and the like. • Plot your current growth in a linear way. Will the needs of your constituency be solved in ten, fifteen, fifty, or more years at your current growth rate? Work out the consequences.
Integrate Rewards and Awards Greenpeace's Dog's Bollocks Award (see Chapter Six) and the Council on Foundations' Celebrate Failure Award at their annual dinner.	• What gets rewarded in your organization? Long service? Not rocking the boat? • Do you celebrate achievement? Do you celebrate positive failure? • Who decides who gets awards? Is it just a top-down process?	• Could you link pay to achievement of results? • Could you have an annual awards ceremony for "greatest failure"? • Could you give people peer-awarded random prizes or gifts for achievement?

Today Kataria holds club sessions across India, often on beaches, where people can practice up to twenty-seven different kinds of laughter linked to breathing exercises. He also organizes laughter sessions in the workplace. A long-term project involves a motorcycle factory, where the managers claim productivity has actually risen by 20 percent since Kataria started running regular laughter sessions for the workers three years ago. (Note that the company isn't making the motorbikes in a different way, just changing workers' *attitudes* toward making them.)

Recently laughter sessions have been held at Bombay's Central Prison. There, prisoners on remand are encouraged to laugh and pull faces as part of a serious program to reduce tension and help them respond positively to their situation. Guards are also encouraged to use laughter as a way to reduce their tension.

Employ a jester. Paul Birch, who worked as a cabin steward for British Airways (BA), took the business of humor a big step further. He wrote to the then chairman of BA, Lord Marshall, to ask if he could have a new role as corporate jester to the company. His business case was that the organization was too staid and conventional and so wasn't capable of responding quickly and creatively to the big changes in the airline world. There wasn't, he maintained, a questioning culture. Amazingly, Lord Marshall agreed to the idea and gave Birch a brief to become BA's corporate fool. A key part of his brief was to challenge existing ways of thinking and doing things. He could challenge anyone—no matter how senior—with immunity. He would "disrupt" board meetings, create wild events, and write poems and songs about business issues.

Birch's ideas are based on an ancient and well-established medieval tradition of the fool or jester. A medieval jester had the right to challenge the king or members of the court and would often encourage people to question their assumptions. Similarly, Birch had the right to challenge anyone in BA—and did so. He and coauthor Brian Clegg (1998) wrote a book about the experiment and its impact and some subsequent work he did. We can summarize his ideas into five rules for any organization brave enough to contemplate having a corporate jester. They appear in "Rules for a Corporate Jester."

Rules for a Corporate Jester

- The jester should not be part of the line management structure and should report to no one.

- The jester should be clear about what's off-limits, if there are limits.

- The jester should use jokes, stories, examples, and metaphors rather than management analysis to challenge ideas.

- The jester should be immune from prosecution (and abuse).

- The jester has to be a full-time jester and can't combine the role with other duties.

Let's be honest. Not many companies have jesters. And it would be hard for a nonprofit to justify such a role to donors. But we think the concept is a useful one. You may well have someone on the staff or the board who can play that challenging role for a time or for a specific activity. It's worth thinking about these questions:

- Do you have a part-time corporate fool—someone who can ask the challenging questions or the questions that no one has thought to ask? If you don't have one, could you ask someone to take on the job for a while?

- If you did appoint someone, perhaps for a meeting, how could he or she work? Would the jester upturn principles or challenge individuals?

- How do others react in your organization when someone tries to play this role and challenge authority? Is he or she encouraged or isolated?

Summary

Achieving a breakthrough requires a mixture of creativity and inno-vation. At various times and in various situations, you will need a balance of each process. The creativity and innovation matrix is a powerful way to establish where you and your competitors are cur-rently. It's also a good way to plot where you'd like to be or need to be at some point in the future.

To be innovative is not easy. And there are few examples in the nonprofit world of organizations that are able to show that innova-tion is an integral part of their culture. One outstanding example in the for-profit world is 3M. They are worth studying because:

- Their innovation track record goes back almost 100 years.
- They have innovation built into their mission statement, reward systems, and business method.

But there also are good nonprofit examples, for example, Green-peace and Amnesty International. At a personal level, individuals also can make a positive difference in established thinking. Consider how you could use the idea of a corporate fool.

Action

If you haven't done so already, plot your organization on the cre-ativity and innovation matrix. Now plot where you want to be, and think about how to get there. What would be the advantages and disadvantages of the new box? What about the risks on the journey?

How could you *embed* creativity and innovation in your culture? How could you create a program to do this and build on 3M's four key principles?

There are a number of ways you can improve creativity and innovation in your organization. These can operate at the level of the organization, board, or team. To improve *creativity*:

- Organize some training in creativity.
- Have "days" given over to creativity.
- Have a special unit whose job is to encourage creativity.
- Appoint an individual—a jester or an artist, for example—to promote creativity and challenge ideas.
- Ask one or more individuals to be responsible for creativity.
- Try to make your work environment more stimulating (see Chapter Eleven).
- Build a culture in which failure—but not poor performance—is welcomed.
- Ask a local arts organization to come in and work with you on creativity.

If you specifically want to improve your *innovation*:

- Benchmark yourself against other organizations in terms of performance.
- Once you've identified the high-performing organizations, identify what it is about their practice that is good—and borrow it.
- Set up challenge grants to encourage innovation.
- Organize job swaps with similar organizations.
- Organize job swaps with dissimilar organizations.
- Promote innovation awards at your annual staff conference.

All of these tactics can work. You don't need to do all of them—but do some!

Chapter Nine

Challenging Mind-Sets

Getting Rid of the Creativity and Innovation Killers

What does the word *mind-set* suggest to you? Typically, people come up with words like *fixed, blocked, narrow, uncreative,* or *limited.* A mind-set can be all those things. A typical definition is "a way of thinking that artificially constrains possibilities." This definition is not completely accurate, however. Of course there are negative and constraining mind-sets, and they should be avoided. But there are also positive and empowering mind-sets that must be cultivated. In our experience, simply eliminating the negative ones isn't enough, especially if you want to work on a breakthrough.

This chapter looks at these different kinds of mind-sets. It shows how to learn to identify and overcome unhelpful mind-sets and gives advice and ideas on how to build up or develop the positive ones. The chapter goes on to contrast two conflicting management philosophies: MBWA (Management by Walking Around) and MBWO (Management by Walking Outside). We argue that MBWO is more suitable for breakthrough mind-sets. Finally we look at how unusual alliances can help to break mind-sets.

Disempowering Mind-Sets

We all have mind-sets. No doubt the human brain is wired such that we have a propensity to create them. The tendency, mentioned earlier, to form general principles from small amounts of data is sometimes useful—don't touch hot stoves—and sometimes unhelpful. Certainly mind-sets have been around for centuries. For example, in the seventeenth century, South Sea Islanders thought they were the only people in the world, as they had had no contact with the developing parts of Europe and Asia. In their worldview, there were only them and the gods. So when Captain Cook arrived, some assumed he was a god because he was so unlike them. They saw his arrival as the fulfillment of an ancient myth. It was their mind-set that made them interpret the data about the color of his skin, his arrival on a ship unlike any they had ever seen, and his technology as evidence of divinity. And that mind-set, as we know, had unfortunate consequences for them. . . .

On a personal level, we sometimes say to ourselves, "I'm not good at giving speeches," and then when we deliver a speech nervously we say to ourselves or others, "See, I told you so." We can come out of the house in the morning and be splashed with mud by a passing car. We have a choice to say, "Things happen . . ." or to say "Oh no, it's going to be one of those days." By choosing a mind-set—consciously or unconsciously—we set ourselves up for how we will interpret or feel about the rest of the day. Notice that many mind-sets are based on taking a very small amount of data—one example, maybe—and building a generalized and often misleading worldview from that. Mind-sets can lead to a variety of limiting behaviors:

- They may cause us to *accept certain explanations to be the case and miss alternatives*. For example, some scientists dismissed Einstein's Theory of Relativity because they *assumed* Newton was right. The obvious, small-scale data supported Newton's theories. What the scientific doubters missed was the big picture that was Einstein's focus. He wasn't concerned with apples falling from trees. He was concerned that when the apple was the size of, say, Jupiter, the kinds of calculations that Newton made didn't work.

- They may cause us to consistently *miss or delete certain kinds of data* even though the data are present. Let's give you a simple, practical example. Look quickly at your watch now and see what time it is. Now, without looking again, try to remember how the "half-past" symbol is shown. Is it a numeral 6, a VI, a line, or what? If you don't know, you have a mind-set that deletes information you think is obvious. Now think about a political party you don't like. Have you ever noticed that every time members of that party do something you don't like you are able to say "Ah ha!" because their actions prove your view? And every time they do something good— and they do—you tend to dismiss that as token or opportunistic.

•   Mind-sets may cause us not to *really see other people's point of view*. For example, look at Figure 9.1. What do you see in the figure? Now ask someone else what he or she sees. Do the two of you agree? Now ask a third and fourth person. What do they see? Even when you come to recognize what others see, do you regard it as "an opinion," or their point of view, but not really *right?* (Some people see a bird, a swan, a phoenix, a beach ball, or a question mark. It could be any of these!)

The ability to really see an alternative point of view is a key one, and one that helps you identify and deal with your own mind-sets. The following quotation, which has been attributed to philosophers from Sartre to Bertrand Russell, illustrates how the same person can have wildly differing ways of interpreting commitment to a point of view.

I *am principled*, you *are stubborn*, he *is prejudiced*.

Figure 9.1   What Do You See?

Clearly mind-sets can have a negative impact on our work and our attempts at breakthrough, in one or more of the following ways:

- We may assume that it's not possible for us to achieve a certain kind of result, whether it's conquering cancer or doubling our membership.
- We may believe that we can only achieve a certain level of performance, that our customers/users/donors won't respond in certain ways, or that colleagues are incapable of delivering certain results.
- We may assume that certain organizations or individuals who affect our work can't change. We may think, for example, "The government will never support our program; it's too radical."
- We may believe that some social context or issue is fixed and can't change—for example, that the law on euthanasia can't change or that "the poor will always be with us."
- We may believe that some social attitude is fixed—"Women will always be oppressed by men" or "The general public will never really appreciate contemporary dance."

If any of these things were unchangeable or "true," they would certainly constrain our ability to set or achieve breakthrough goals. But how unchangeable or true are they? This chapter encourages you to *identify* and *question* your mind-sets.

How Do We Form Mind-Sets?

We form mind-sets in different ways. Some are just *prejudices* we pick up from others—for example, a distrust of other races or cultures. Some are *culturally or socially given*—for example, the obsession with women's thinness in some Western societies. Some are the product of *experience*, as in "We've always done it this way."

One other way we form mind-sets is by *implication* or *inference*. Chris Argyris (1982) explores this idea, showing how as individuals

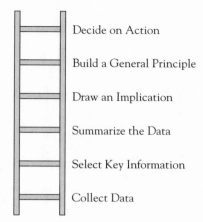

Decide on Action

Build a General Principle

Draw an Implication

Summarize the Data

Select Key Information

Collect Data

Figure 9.2   The Ladder of Implication

we can take the same piece of data, interpret it differently from other people, draw different implications from the data, then draw fundamentally different conclusions about people and the world, and finally take very different action based on those conclusions. The challenge is we may draw inappropriate or inaccurate conclusions and then take inappropriate action. Our conclusions can then become very unhelpful mind-sets for us, the people we work with, the audience we serve, the competitors we have, the way we have to work, and so on. Figure 9.2 adapts Argyris's ladder metaphor (1982) to illustrate this process.

Let's go through an example to see how the process can work. Fred, Barney, and Wilma are having a debate on how to pay for the breakthrough needed in the quality of social care provided in society. They're trying to decide if it's best done through voluntary individual giving or through mandatory taxes levied by the government. Table 9.1 on page 180 shows how each person comes to his or her different conclusions. (Read the table from the bottom up.) Notice that the data at the bottom are the same.

Fred is someone who believes that, generally, governments should provide social infrastructure. Barney is someone who, in general, believes less government is best. Fred looks at the neutral data

Table 9.1 Same Data, Different Actions: Ladder of Implication

Ladder Step	Fred	Barney	Wilma
Decide on Action	For there to be decent social care, it needs to be paid for from government taxes.	We should first look to the community to provide social care.	We should have a balance of methods.
Build a General Principle	Not enough people care about the community.	Most people care about the community.	We need to educate people *and* ensure a safety net.
Draw an Implication	A significant number of people don't give to good causes.	The great majority of people are keen to help good causes.	There's a big split in society.
Summarize the Data	A significant number of people are stingy.	Most people are generous.	There are different views on charity giving.
Select Key Information	15% of people don't regularly give to charity.	85% of people give regularly to charity.	15% don't give; 85% do.
Collect Data	In a survey, 85% of people say they give regularly to charity, and 15% say they don't.		

and forms a series of conclusions based on his initial selection of one piece of information—that 15 percent of people don't regularly give to charity. He concludes that governments need to tax to meet social care needs. Barney works with the same neutral data but focuses on the fact that 85 percent of people *do* give regularly to charity. He then concludes that the answer is for the community to pay for social care. Wilma takes a more pragmatic and open view than either Fred or Barney. By avoiding either mind-set, she can cope with the two opinions sitting side by side. She opts for a mixture of government and local community care. The same neutral data actually allow three people to draw radically different *conclusions* based on different *interpretations*.

You can use the ladder when you're trying to help a group understand its mind-sets. Use it to work back from group members' conclusions about preferred actions to the data that make them think that way. Or if the group is starting with a set of data, use the ladder as a way of helping the members reach a balanced conclusion. For example, produce a statistic and then ask three groups to go away and come up with conclusions about it. How about "80 percent of aid to African countries is wasted"? What different implications could be drawn?

To get some practice, you can try to work out the missing steps in the ladder shown in Table 9.2. Once you've done that, see if there's a different way to interpret the data or a different conclusion you could draw.

Ways to Challenge Mind-Sets in Organizations

Of course it's not just individuals who have mind-sets. Organizations do too. And these can be just as constraining. There are a number of ways to challenge mind-sets in organizations.

Create a Debate

You can ask two colleagues to prepare opposite points of view on a proposition and encourage others to listen to them in a debate format. Begin by recording people's views on the topic at the start of

Table 9.2   Ladder Exercise

	Case A	Case B
Decide on Action	We should fundraise only from individuals for our theatre program.	We should hire only women.
Build a General Principle		
Draw an Implication		
Summarize the Data		
Collect Data	90% of corporations say they expect to gain preferential benefits from sponsorship of arts organizations.	Only 1 in 20 top nonprofit jobs is held by a woman.

the debate and then ask them to record their views at the end. This debate technique is often used to great effect at the International Fund Raising Congress in Holland, where almost one thousand of the world's top fundraisers gather each year to improve their fundraising practice. They use it on such topics as "We should take more corporate money." The purpose of the debate is to ensure that the issue is discussed vigorously to help improve everyone's thinking. In 2000, they actually hired an automatic voting system for a major plenary session, and before the plenary started they asked delegates to rate the value of key characteristics, such as leadership, belief, emotion, and the like, in transforming fundraising. Ten speakers put forward their case for the value of different qualities. At the end, everyone was asked to vote again to see if their opinions had changed. Remarkably, perhaps, people did change their views quite a lot. This debate technique is also the approach famously used at Harvard Business School where students are asked to prepare different ways to analyze a business situation, for example, what's the best thing to do from the board's point of view, or from the CEO's perspective, or from the shareholders' point of view.

To create a debate, set up a challenging proposition, such as "We can recruit ten thousand new members within six months." Ask different teams to present their case—not in a balanced or reasonable way but polemically as they feel inclined. Alternatively, if you're feeling very creative, you could ask the key *opponent* of the idea to *propose* it and the key *backer* of the idea to *oppose* it. The end result is likely to be a well thought out and balanced argument.

Use a Corporate Jester

This technique (discussed in Chapter Eight) involves appointing, perhaps temporarily, a person to challenge opinions and ideas, especially those of senior people. The jester can be an internal or external person. For example, an outside consultant can be a good, disinterested party to have ask not just the unaskable but also the deceptively simple.

The "fool" is allowed to ask irreverent and perhaps even seemingly irrelevant questions. And he or she can ask them of anyone. The jester might challenge accepted ways of doing things even by just asking Why? Note that for a fool to be effective, he or she has to be able to do whatever is necessary without sanction.

Use Drama and Creativity

An increasingly popular technique in a number of organizations is to hire actors or theatre companies to explore a topic, usually in front of staff teams. Positions, roles, and issues can be explored in a way that makes a serious conflict manageable. And the actors, as part of their research, are able to help identify mind-sets in a safe way. (See the passage on Hewlett-Packard and the Equal Opportunities Commission.)

Hold a Sacred Cow Barbecue

One way to challenge mind-sets is to identify them as sacred cows and then see if you should sacrifice them on a barbecue. This is really a metaphor for thinking the unthinkable. The actual technique is very straightforward. You simply write down on Post-its things you wouldn't or couldn't do as an organization. The Post-its are then stuck up on a flipchart to be discussed or debated. The sacred cows could be things like "charge for our services" or "take money from an oil company." We recently held such a barbecue with the board of Amnesty International, who wanted to craft a new strategic direction. To get some food at the barbecue, board members had to put forward an "unthinkable thought" for consideration. The ideas were then "saved" or "cooked."

One general example of a sacred cow challenge recently imported from the United States to the United Kingdom is private sector management of public services. For a long time it was regarded as impossible for schools and prisons in the United Kingdom to be run by private corporations. Now both practices are common, if not universally welcomed. Similarly, senior staff at a major U.K. cancer charity had a vigorous internal discussion about whether or not to give its support to a cigarette that contained a vaccine designed to immunize young women against a virus that causes cervical cancer. (Young women are the fastest-growing group of smokers *and* the age group most at risk—because of their level of sexual activity—of catching the virus.) Previously, such an idea would have been dismissed out of hand. In the end they decided to look at other ways to deliver the vaccine. But the debate was real and challenging, and it opened up previously unexplored territory for the charity.

Let's be clear that looking at getting rid of sacred cows is not the same as getting rid of your values. Organizations *need* to have values and beliefs. These values and beliefs form a vital part of the way they operate. If you're an anti-gun organization, you're unlikely to take money from the NRA, however tempting the package. But it's important that you work through exactly *why* you wouldn't do something and what the advantages would be if you did. You may well end up with a more profound affirmation of your values. You may also come to recognize that some of the positions you adopt as an organization are not really *values* but simply established ways of doing things.

Set Boundaries on How to Break Rules

Challenging mind-sets can involve breaking rules. Curiously, you need to set rules on when and how to break rules. At =mc we often invoke what we call the *champagne rules* when working with customers. These rules are brought into play when we spend time with a top team thinking the unthinkable. Here they are:

- Anyone can say anything.
- No one is to make personal attacks, and no challenges will be taken personally.
- No challenging remarks will be repeated outside the meeting.
- Only things the group has agreed to take forward will be recorded. Everything else will be forgotten.

Why champagne? Because people say wild things when drunk on champagne . . . and the next morning it's best to forget most of it—but not all.

Readers' Theatres and Christmas Shows

In the 1990s, Hewlett-Packard created a system of "readers' theatres." Staff would create a play based on some topic they felt strongly about and that they wanted to share with colleagues. The play was then read out (hence the name) in front of colleagues. This technique is quite different from running a focus group or a survey.

Readers' theatre was used to change the HP senior management mind-set on gay and lesbian rights. The company had originally decided not to offer benefits to partners of gay and lesbian employees. Despite the fact HP had a history of liberal benefits, there was a mind-set about this particular issue. Some employees created a drama illustrating how the decision discriminated unfairly and produced unjust hardship. Senior management saw the play and, reflecting on the harsh implications of their policy, reversed their decision.

In the United Kingdom, the Equal Opportunities Commission, the national agency responsible for ensuring that equal opportunities legislation is implemented, also used drama internally.

Ocassionally, staff produced a pantomime—a special Christmas comic show—that highlighted their issues and concerns. Using humor, they were able to explore topics that revealed internal tensions on a whole range of issues—pay, seniority, decision making—in a way that confounded the normal hierarchy. The show was an effective but nonthreatening way of challenging the status quo.

Ask Questions

Almost by definition, making a breakthrough will require that your organization change its mind-sets. To begin that process, you can ask yourself and your colleagues at your organization the following six questions:

1. What's the *ideal situation* we aspire to? What does it look like? How does it feel? How would we describe it in words?

2. What's the *key challenge* in achieving this goal? Can we make it more specific and concrete?

3. Is there *really* a problem about achieving this goal or taking this action? What's the underlying concern? Is the problem becoming more or less serious?

4. Are we making *assumptions* about the size, scope, or intractability of the problem? Are there other ways to view this problem? How do others see it?

5. Have we made any *self-limiting assumptions* about our resources or capabilities? Have we made any self-limiting assumptions about others' resources or capabilities?

6. What do we *really want* in this situation? What are our aims and desired outcomes? Do we agree as a team or organization about those?

Comfort Zones and Self-Limiting Beliefs

One particular kind of mind-set is called a comfort zone (see also Chapter Two). A comfort zone is a set of parameters within which we are content to operate, a level of performance that feels safe. When working in the comfort zone, we have a rationale for not dramatically improving our performance—that is, achieving breakthrough success.

Comfort zones can be both personal and professional. For example, you might say, "Well, I can't get into my 30-inch trousers, but at least I don't have to wear 36s like some people." So you settle for the comfort zone of 32-inch trousers. *Actually* you'd love to get into 30s, but the avoidance of having to go up to 36s makes 32s acceptable. Or you might say, "I earn $45K. That's not as much as I'd like, but I can live on it, and it's more than others earn." So you never go for that raise or for that higher-paying or riskier job.

In a work setting, a charity might say, "Well, we improved our income by 7 percent last year. That wasn't as good as the top charity, but not as bad as the worst." So the managers and staff feel content. Or, "We'll never get the majority of people in the country to be concerned about HIV and AIDS, so there's no point in really trying to go for mass appeal. We'll have to stay a marginal cause." Or a university is happy that it's in the upper half of the academic league table in a particular subject. Internally, the academic staff and administration accept that the university is never going to be the best. Or members of a theatre company are content to perform to 75 percent capacity instead of 100 percent. They only feel dissatisfaction if the audience drops to 50 percent. These are all examples of comfort zones—that is, the organization or key individuals in it have internalized and accepted an unremarkable level of performance.

Creative Organizations Get Uncreative

Arts and cultural organizations apply incredible creativity to their artistic work, but they often struggle to do the same with their management or operations.

We were working with a theatre in the north of England that had an aim of being able to charge a flat fee of just $8 for a seat. This goal of $8 a seat was a sacred tenet. (Prices currently ran from $10 to $45.) When the theatre wasn't full, the price of seats was invoked as the reason. Underpinning the $8 goal were the following beliefs:

- We have a duty to bring theatre to everyone.

- The main barrier to participation in theatre—especially by disadvantaged people—is cost.

- It is the duty of the local government to give the theatre enough money to keep prices low.

- Fewer poor or disadvantaged people come to the theatre because prices are too high.

We accepted the first belief (though there is also a case for arguing that it's OK for theatre to be elitist). We also did some research into the local economy and what other leisure or entertainment outlets were available. This included looking at the supporters of the local soccer team, soccer being traditionally a sport favored by disadvantaged and poor people. Here is what we discovered:

- The average wage in the town was $25,000 per year.

- The average soccer fan earned slightly less than the average wage ($20,000).

- The average soccer fan had to pay $1,800 to support the team: $700 for a season ticket, $400 for merchandise, and $700 for fees for premium games.

Our conclusion was that if the people of the city really *care* about what you do, *they will pay*. We challenged the theatre's mind-set: "It's

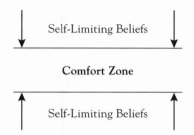

**Figure 9.3   How Self-Limiting Beliefs
and Comfort Zones Relate**

not the price of what you do; it's the way people feel about it." In
response to this challenge, the theatre

- Ran focus groups with soccer fans to find out what they were
  interested in.
- Went to some soccer games themselves to experience the
  "magic."
- Reworked their artistic program.
- Copied a number of practices from the soccer club.
- Put on a show about soccer!

As we said, comfort zones represent an area of safe performance
for an individual or organization. Unfortunately, comfort zones can
too easily become reinforced and rigidified by *self-limiting beliefs*
(SLBs). When this happens, the comfort lulls us into maintaining
low expectations and limiting what we believe is possible. Figure
9.3 illustrates how SLBs and comfort zones relate to each other.

We've given some examples of how SLBs constrain both individuals and organizations. To *really* succeed—to *break through*—all
of us need to learn to articulate our SLBs and then get rid of them.
Here we've given you a couple of examples of personal SLBs and
how they constrain the person who holds them. What are your
SLBs, and what negative effect do they have on you? You might
want to make your own chart.

Some SLBs I Have About Myself	*How These Constrain Me*
I don't have a university education.	I could never become a CEO— you need a degree.
I'll always earn about the average.	I'll never be able to hold an intellectual conversation.
I'm a woman, and women aren't treated fairly in a man's world.	I'll never get through the glass ceiling.
Men will always try to oppress me, so I must be on my guard.	I need to adopt more manlike attitudes to succeed.

Now think about your *organization*. Common organizational SLBs include the following:

> Our cause will never be as popular as the environment [or children, animals, and the like].
>
> We don't have the resources to grow as big as Nonprofits X, Y, and Z.
>
> Headquarters doesn't understand the reality for us here in the local branches.
>
> The people in the local branches don't understand the big picture.

What SLBs does your organization have? How do these constrain its operations and activities? You might want to make another chart on which to write down your ideas.

SLBs constrain you and your organization in various ways. For each SLB there are at least two levels of implication. The first concerns how the SLB will constrain your potential for breakthrough *now*. The second relates to how it will constrain your potential for breakthrough in the *future*.

Let's take an example, such as "Headquarters doesn't understand the reality for us here in the local branches." This might constrain you *now* as you think

We should treat HQ with suspicion.

It's not worth explaining things to them.

We need to keep information to ourselves.

If you don't do anything about this mind-set, it might get much worse in *three years' time*, when you think

Maybe we should just act like a separate organization.

Let's cover up things that have gone wrong—headquarters will only make trouble.

We should give information to headquarters only if they ask a direct question.

Usually negative mind-sets get worse—and create worse situations. You need to tackle them now.

Adopt Powerful Enabling Mind-Sets

As we said at the beginning of this chapter, not all mind-sets are negative and disempowering; some are positive and enabling. Your first step is to identify yours as one or the other. We've talked a bit about recognizing and getting rid of negative mind-sets, but getting rid of them is not enough. You've got to replace them with positive, powerful, enabling mind-sets.

This strategy of creating positive mind-sets is common in the sports world. Think, for a moment, of Muhammad Ali. Born black and poor in the racist South in the 1940s, he *could* have internalized the oppression and the negative mind-set all around him about his chances of lifting himself up from there. Instead, he chose to create his own *positive* mind-set and to express it in a catchphrase. At the age of sixteen he began to say, "I am the greatest." Notice that he

Said it in the *present* tense—as though it were true *now*

Made it *positive and affirmative*

Made it contain a *breakthrough goal*

Didn't specify *how*, but focused on the *what*

Of course, Ali had to subsequently develop a specific strategy about how to achieve his goal.

We can't all be Muhammad Ali. But we *can* all use this pattern to formulate for ourselves the positive mind-sets needed for breakthrough. Let's be clear about something, though: we are not talking about simply saying

"We can do anything."

"Just do it."

"Just develop Positive Mental Attitude (PMA)."

The "just do it" and "PMA" mentalities are not really enough. "Just do it" can imply not thinking through the implications of what one does. And in an nonprofit setting, the values behind people's actions and the impact of what they do are important. You *can* say, "Let's take action having accounted for some reasonable risks . . ."

Equally bad is simplistic PMA. Some people say PMA itself is enough. You just need to go into any situation with a positive approach. Well, we've wandered around Chicago with a positive mental attitude on a wet and windy afternoon trying to find a building, sure it was "just a few blocks further on." After two hours, one of us said to the other, "Why don't we get a map or ask someone? It's not enough simply to positively maintain that the building must be around here somewhere. And if the current wandering around strategy doesn't work, we need to adopt a different strategy." Point made? You need maps—or a strategy—to succeed. A positive and enabling mind-set can take many forms and can be achieved in a range of ways, some of which are outlined later in the chapter. Typically, however, this positive and enabling mind-set will involve:

- A clear, concrete, and energizing goal
- A strategy or a number of strategies to achieve the goal
- The flexibility to adapt strategies

Reframing

One way to gain a positive and useful mind-set and to acquire some ideas or strategies is through *reframing*. In reframing we begin by accepting the reality of the negative mind-set and then looking for the positive alternative actions or strategy to counter that negative mind-set. Here are some examples. Notice that in each case it is necessary that:

- You accept the initial negative premise, even if it's not true.
- You generate a number of alternative actions or strategies to deal with the negative premise.
- You look for a specific positive implication of the premise.

Potential SLBs	Reframes
Headquarters doesn't understand us.	Yes, but that means we have a fantastic opportunity to help them understand and should work on that through exchange visit and so on.
	Yes, but that means they give us independence since they recognize we're different. How can we make the most of that?
	Yes, but we can work with other regional offices to try to build a real sense of what we need to achieve. Let's do that.

We're a small child-care organization and can never be as big as UNICEF.	Yes, but we are flexible because we're small and should build on that flexibility.
	Yes, but we're really in touch with the children we serve and should think about how we can feed that perception and knowledge into larger agencies.
	Yes, but we don't have to have a big bureaucracy to succeed and should concentrate on maintaining our level of efficiency.
We're an unpopular cause because we're concerned with helping former drug dealers get back into work.	Yes, but our supporters really understand and are committed to our cause, so we should look at how to build on that.
	Yes, but we're learning lessons that might be useful to others about how to sell challenging ideas. Let's see how we can share those techniques.
	Yes, but we're making a vital contribution to the well-being of this city and should focus on selling our wider benefit.

Now think about how to reframe some of your SLBs as positives.

Transforming Mind-Sets: Bridging the Digital Divide

There's a lot of talk about the digital divide—the way in which developed countries deliberately or unintentionally maintain their power over developing countries through their use of IT. But there are some fantastic examples of groups and organizations in developing countries using IT and the Internet to bridge the divide. The Wapishama tribe in Guyana have bridged that divide and also changed their mind-sets about the value of their work.

For good or for ill, the Wapishama have gradually come in contact with Western money and industrialized goods. They have been able to afford to buy some goods, such as textiles, but others, like a tractor to improve their crops, have seemed out of reach. And some Western goods, like computers, have seemed irrelevant to their way of life. This contact with the West has produced some challenges for the tribe. For example, Wapishama women have been weaving hammocks from exquisite rainforest cotton for hundreds of years. Each hammock requires almost six hundred hours of work to create. The skill almost died out ten years ago when warmer and cheaper manufactured blankets became available locally. But then a young volunteer, Matthew Squire of Voluntary Service Overseas (a U.K. nonprofit), encouraged the women to begin weaving again. He brought back samples to the United Kingdom, and both the British Royal Family and the British Museum bought one as artwork for several hundred dollars. The money was gratefully received, but it wasn't enough to buy the tractor.

Inspired by implications of this initial success, however, the Guyana Telephone and Telegraph Company donated $12,000 of computers and provided a webmaster, Sharla Hernandez, to help set up a promotional website about the tribe's crafts and, in particular, their hammocks. Through the website, the tribe began to sell the hammocks—a lot of them. Some PR coverage in the *New York Times* provided a further spur, and within a few months the tribe had enough money to buy the tractor they had wanted for some time.

Now they're looking at ways to expand their sales so that they can both maintain their traditions *and* become more self-sufficient.

Changing Organizational Mind-Sets: MBWA Versus MBWO

Often organizations find it difficult to come up with an *internal* stimulus for their breakthrough idea or to tackle mind-sets. They then need to look for *outside* stimuli. However, the question can arise, "What is outside?" Let's contrast two management ideas—each with a different definition of outside, and both useful in different ways. The two ideas are managing by walking around (MBWA) and managing by walking outside (MBWO).

MBWA was created in reaction to the fact that many senior managers of large organizations had for some time been trapped inside their ivory management towers, out of touch with the reality of customers and ordinary staff, staring off into the strategic distance. What was needed, the MBWA philosophy maintains, was for the managers to get out of their offices and meet and find out about internal and external customers. (*Internal customers* is the MBWA term for organizational staff and colleagues.) Many organizations began with the external customers, trying to get closer to them and find out more about them and their interests, through customer surveys and the like, and trying to discover how the organization and its processes were perceived. The MBWA (get-closer-to-the-customer) approach was touted by management gurus like Tom Peters. It was hugely influential in the private sector and subsequently in the public and nonprofit sectors.

The MBWA phenomenon did have good outcomes. In the commercial world it led to interesting developments. For external customers, it led to a more serious and fundamental approach to customer care and service. But it also had some interesting developments in terms of internal customers, too. In the U.K., a hugely popular TV show, "Back to the Shop Floor," was launched in which senior executives agreed to work for a week in low-paid, front-line jobs in their own organizations. In the series, surgeons became hospital porters, newspaper editors became cub reporters, and the CEO of Burger King sold burgers and fries for eight hours a day.

- Michael Eisner, the world's highest-paid executive, is rumored to have agreed to work in one of the Disney theme parks one day a year—selling food, collecting rubbish, or selling tickets—to find out how customers really felt about the Disney experience.

- The mayor of Bangkok swept the streets for one day a month over an entire year to find out how ordinary Bangkok citizens viewed the city.

- The idea of customer connection also had an impact on the office environment. Many organizations saw their CEOs move into the open-plan office, and some organizations even had one big table where everyone sat.

All of these initiatives were good *and* had the effect of bringing senior managers closer to the reality of both internal and external customers.

This approach had a massive impact in the nonprofit world too:

- Mike Aaronson, director general of Save the Children (SCF) U.K., pledged to spend more of his time in the field and not at his desk. His extended visits to projects all over the world gave him, he believed, a much fuller understanding and appreciation of the work of SCF than reading reports in his London office could ever do.

- The Ford Foundation opened offices in other countries to avoid being too U.S.-centric. It developed a much more rounded policy that clearly reflected the needs and interests of the other countries as a result of the input from these offices.

- A number of development charities sent new members of their fundraising staff overseas to visit projects. Previously the norm had been to wait until a staff member had worked with the charity for two years. The result of this change was that instead of seeing the trip as a "reward" for being with the nonprofit for two years, staff saw firsthand the work of their organization and came back inspired to do even better.

- The director of social services for a large London borough
  answered calls directly at the emergency advice desk for one
  day a month. He then understood—or remembered from his
  own early career—the kinds of challenges and stresses his
  front liners faced.

So there are good results from the MBWA approach, but there
are some downsides to MBWA, too. These are not strictly *negative*
mind-sets, but they are certainly limiting mind-sets. It can lead you
to focus too closely on *current* customers or users and thus miss
emerging groups. And where do you go when you're as close to your
customer as you can get? Or if, as sometimes happens, the customer
simply seems to want more of the same? MBWA can also create a
certain introverted feedback loop where the people you wander
around with start to reinforce your existing views. This is when the
mind-sets can start to kick in.

Too Close to the Customer?

Network—a pseudonym—is one of the United Kingdom's leading
charities working with people with a specific learning difficulty and
their caregivers. In the 1990s it went through a major democratization process, involving people with cerebral palsy and their parents
more closely in the management of the charity.

Not long after this carefully engineered democratization process,
Network began to have some extremely serious financial troubles in
the mid-1990s, exacerbated by a number of changes in CEO. There
was an urgent need to cut costs and specifically to close some resi-
dential care settings.

The problem was, of course, that the high level of user involvement in management—in itself a good thing—created massive con-
flicts and challenges when it came to making cuts to services that
directly affected the individuals involved or their peers. There are
challenges in creating too strong a user-service bond when there is
likely to be a conflict over allocation of resources.

So MBWA isn't enough and may lead to some negative consequences. Sometimes then you have to wander further afield, and that's where MBWO comes in.

MBWO: Looking *Outside* to Challenge Mind-Sets and Bring About Breakthrough

In our breakthrough work we've been encouraging organizations to begin to change from MBWA to *managing by walking outside* (MBWO). The basic idea behind MBWO is that all really radical ideas that have an impact on an industry come from *outside* that industry. That is, the MBWA phenomenon can create *too* warm and fuzzy a relationship about what you do and how you do it. You can't easily challenge all that from within. You're also more likely to get a really radical idea from outside simply because that source is not constrained by perceived limitations of the existing possibilities. People *inside* the industry—whether it's public, private, or nonprofit—may have a mind-set about what will and won't work. Sometimes it takes someone from *outside* to successfully challenge the received wisdom.

The following are two examples of breakthroughs that came from "outsiders" challenging internal mind-sets in whole industries:

• Steve Jobs and Steve Wozniak of Apple tried to sell their concept of a "friendly personal computer on every desk" to the computer industry. That industry's response was to say, "Why would everyone want to have a computer on his desk? A computer is a big machine that sits in the basement." For major computer manufacturers of the time, at least part of the problem was that Jobs and Wozniak were from outside the computer industry.

• When the cell phone industry began to develop in the United Kingdom, British Telecom wasn't sure whether to get involved. Its argument was, "There are so many fixed line phones and public phones—who needs their own mobile phone apart from a few traveling businesspeople?"

The nonprofit world can be similarly blinkered:

- Bob Geldof, who organized the world's largest and most successful fundraising special event—Live Aid—knew *nothing* about organizing special events or charity fundraising. He broke all the "rules" as laid down by professional fundraising bodies like the Association of Fundraising Professionals. As a result of breaking these rules, he was hugely successful. Now we can learn from him.
- Esther Rantzen was the host of a consumer-rights talk show in the United Kingdom in the 1980s and 1990s. She had an idea for a telephone counseling service that children could call for free. She approached a number of child-care charities to ask them to set it up. A number of senior figures in these charities were skeptical. They said that it would be abused by children making hoax calls, it was too complex, or it wouldn't be used. Besides which, "What does a TV presenter know about telephone counseling?"

They had missed the point. Ignoring the "expert" advice, Rantzen set up an nonprofit called Childline, and it has turned into one of the most successful children's telephone advice charities in the United Kingdom.

Do You Need to Be an Expert to Transform Something?

Fender is a legend in the world of rock guitars. An engineer-entrepreneur, Leo Fender invented—and then figured out how to mass produce and market—the solid body electric guitar.

He started his working life as a radio repairman in California, fixing amplifiers. In the mid-1940s he began to design guitars and came up with the radical Telecaster (1948). This was adored by musicians for its clean performance and lack of feedback (but scorned by other manufacturers for its bolt-on neck and slab body).

In the 1950s Fender went on to invent the two guitars that became the fantasy object of every real and aspiring rock musician the world over: the Precision solid body electric guitar (1951) and—the all-time classic—the Stratocaster (1954).

Fender died in 1991 at the age of eighty-two. Despite his enormous contribution to rock music, *Fender never learned to play the guitar.* You don't need to be able to do the process yourself to transform its performance.

The following are some examples of how organizations are increasingly using MBWO to bring in external stimuli:

• A U.K. charity telephone fundraising team went to visit First Direct, the world's first telephone banking service, to find out how it maintained high levels of customer feedback. As a result, they developed new skills in "reading" conversations, developing sales lines, and even using data mining.

• Honda famously bought ten thousand cockroaches to study their ability to accelerate quickly and their interesting suspension, which enables them to get in and out of strange spaces. What for? To radically challenge their approach to and current thinking on car design.

• Mckinsey, the international consulting firm, took all its key staff—almost five thousand—to a small Italian island and hired a number of artists to help them produce an opera in five days. The purpose? To learn from the world of the arts how to manage big messy projects. The firm wanted to reverse the "business knows best" mind-set among the staff.

What external stimuli can you bring in to challenge your organization's mind-set to promote MBWO? These suggestions might give you some ideas:

• As an aid agency, talk to a travel company about how to efficiently move large numbers of people and baggage out from the home country. See how you could adopt the methods that work best.

• As a school, visit a theatre to find out how they unlock actors' creativity through improvisation workshops. Apply a similar technique with students.

- As a fundraiser, study porn sites on the Net (they're still the most successful sites). Identify how some of their techniques could improve your Net-based fundraising efforts.

Experiencing Oppression to Understand It

We were working with an environmental nonprofit in Canada that wanted us to tackle how to promote a more sophisticated view and how issues of oppression and equal opportunities were dealt with in its workplace.

They had a really excellent, hundred-page manual on equal opportunities and diversity, and they had organized diversity training. However, neither the manual nor the training seemed to be having the strong cultural impact the organization wanted. The nonprofit's management still felt the staff didn't really understand how people felt when they were oppressed or discriminated against.

We asked a staff group the question, "How do for-profits change culture?" In the middle of a whole list of brainstormed ideas came the phrase *dress-down Friday,* used by corporations to introduce a more relaxed approach in the workplace. This agency really couldn't have a more relaxed dress code. Nevertheless, the staff took the concept and built on it to develop a whole new idea relevant to them and their desire for radical challenge to change their culture. To help change mind-sets, they introduced the idea of cross-dressing Tuesday. On the next four Tuesdays, staff were asked to come to work on public transportation dressed as a member of the opposite sex. In doing this they experienced discrimination and funny looks on the metro and the bus and discovered *something* of what it's like to be odd or outside the norm.

The idea was to give staff members a means of experiencing oppression and difference. They used this experience as part of the discussions and training that followed. The result in the organization's view was the looked-for change in attitude and approach.

By reading these examples, you can see that there are two approaches to MBWO: bringing outsiders in to stir things up and consciously going outside to have different experiences. Once you've identified that you can benefit from external inspiration, be sure to have clear answers to these questions:

- Who should or could we learn from, no matter how different they are from us?
- What's our purpose in seeking the inspiration?
- How will we collect information when we're there?
- How will we analyze the information when we get back?
- How will we implement any new ideas, practices, and processes?

Aid Workers Change Their Mind-Set

Oxfam is an international relief and development agency. They were working with large numbers of refugees in the Caucasus. Aid workers distributed clothing through a system of coupons. The procedure was a bit like wartime rationing in Europe: the refugees had to stand in line and were then given slips of paper with, for example, "3 shirts, 5 pairs of underpants, 1 dress, . . ." written on them. Which items were included on the vouchers was determined using a standard formula based on the number of people in the family. The refugees would then exchange the vouchers for clothes.

From Oxfam's point of view, this was an efficient system that gave people what they needed. Although grateful for the clothes, the refugees perceived the system as yet another reminder of the extent to which their lives were now run by others. They queued up, were assessed, and then received a voucher. They were unhappy.

Oxfam couldn't change the situation the refugees found themselves in, but the workers did want to find some way to give them back some semblance of self-determination. Although there still had to be an assessment, the clothing coupons were replaced with photocopied vouchers in various denominations made to look like "money." Instead of being told what they could have, the refugees could now go to the clothes stalls and choose and "buy" what they needed and wanted for their families. What they bought was very similar to what they had been allocated in the past. The difference was that now they made their own choices, and they felt like customers.

Through changing their organizational mind-set about efficiency, the Oxfam workers had restored some dignity to the refugees.

Build Alliances

As part of the process of making outside connections and changing your personal and organizational mind-sets, you may want to build unusual alliances with other organizations so as to benchmark, to swap staff, to exchange ideas—and to challenge mind-sets. Our experience suggests the more unusual and challenging the alliance, the better.

These are some of the unusual alliances and swaps we've helped organize in the effort to challenge mind-sets:

- An arts organization talking to the U.S. Army about vision, mission, and setting goals to be really clear about outcomes and the resources needed to achieve them
- An environmental charity talking to an oil company about values and beliefs to challenge preconceptions about what motivates people and what they believe is ethical
- A conservative city council talking to a radical campaigning organization about selling the vision internally and the importance of stunts and simple headline messages

Such connections, we've found, are challenging and difficult to manage but ultimately rewarding for both sides. Think about what organizations you could build alliances with and what you and the other organization could get out of the alliance.

Alliances at Work in the Kitchen

Alliances can have powerful mutual benefits. There is now, for example, a strong working relationship between some of the United Kingdom's top restaurants and experimental physicists.

Several top U.K. restaurants, including the Michelin two-star Manoir au Quatre Saisons, are collaborating with the quaintly named International Molecular and Physical Gastronomy Group (IMPEG). IMPEG is a group of top university scientists who also share a passion for fine food. Using physics and molecular biology, the scientists advise the chefs on how to create new—apparently impossible—dishes. Some successes include

Reversed Baked Alaska: this dish, in which ice cream is wrapped around a *hot* sponge cake, was developed by Raymond Blanc, owner of Le Manoir. He was helped by Nicholas Kurti, an Oxford physicist who explored the physics of achieving such a result. Kurti, incidentally, was also involved in creating the atom bomb.

Fig and pineapple jelly: as any cook knows, it's "impossible" to make a jelly from figs or pineapple that actually sets, because of an enzyme these fruits contain. Undeterred by this centuries-old truth, Dr. Peter Borham, a Bristol University scientist, worked with Heston Blumenthal, owner of The Fat Duck restaurant, to solve the problem. Using his grasp of molecular biology, he found a way to counter the enzyme. Fig-pineapple jelly, properly set, is now on the menu.

The apparently light-hearted IMPEG-restaurant collaboration actually has some important implications: unlikely people and disciplines can make connections through shared passions and interests, and the impossible may be possible if you just ask for help from someone else with a different view or perspective.

And it's not just in the rarefied world of haute cuisine that unusual alliances are in operation. Consider the case of Via Voice, one of IBM's hottest products, which allows you to speak into, and even direct, your computer using your voice.

This hugely successful software is likely to be the future of computers, rather than a mouse and keyboard. It was developed partly with the help of disability organizations. Over a number of years, these organizations were given seed grants by IBM as part of its community investment program to try out various methods of controlling computers. For people with disabilities, being able to control computers using something other than the mouse-keyboard combination was a *necessity*. And for many, voice activation was simply the best and most powerful way to do it. The result is software, still being improved, that is able to adapt to various voices and various degrees of distinctiveness. So Via Voice is a commercial breakthrough that owes at least part of its success to nonprofit involvement.

HelpAge Japan (HAJ) is a national nonprofit providing a whole range of services to elders. The enterprising and entrepreneurial head of this nonprofit decided to build some links with the private sector that would directly benefit his users. Over the last decade, he has developed a whole series of partnerships with local engineering firms. They get to tap into various HAJ services to test new engineering ideas, such as for hoists and lift controls that allow someone with little agility in his or her hands to control a large machine using small fingertip controls. In return, the firms act as a useful aid and adaptation service for the users.

Concern, the Irish development charity, established an exchange program with 3M, the company famous for their innovation. The deal was simple: Concern gained insight into 3M's innovation techniques to apply to its work, and 3M gained a strong community investment program.

Summary

Often the reason organizations give for being unable to transform their performance has to do with lack of resources or lack of support from partner agencies or funders. And it's true that this is sometimes the case. But, at least as often, the reason for underachievement or failure to break through has to do with a mental block—a disempowering or negative mind-set at the organizational, staff, or individual level. To really succeed in achieving breakthrough results, you need to work on getting rid of these negative mind-sets and building up positive and empowering ones.

Challenges to mind-sets can take a number of forms:

- Identify the mind-sets you have and establish how they limit your own or your organization's performance. Establish, too, how these mind-sets will limit your performance in the future.
- Check that what started out as a good idea, for example MBWA, hasn't become a limiting mind-set.
- Think about working on a program of MBWO to challenge your or your organization's new approach or culture.
- Build alliances with unusual partners to help achieve the unachievable. Look especially for organizations that share your passion but achieve their goals in a radically different way.

Action

Begin by being clear about any mind-sets that currently exist in yourself, your team, and your organization. Divide these into two groups: those that will help you achieve your breakthrough goal and those that will hold you back.

Remember that the ones that will hold you back may be masquerading as key beliefs or values. Don't be afraid to hold a sacred cow barbecue.

You will almost certainly have to develop some new and empowering beliefs to achieve your breakthrough goal. Consider developing these at the same three levels of self, team, and organization. These beliefs should be specific and concrete, action-orientated, and open to change and adaptation. Try reframing the negative beliefs, if appropriate. Remember reframing requires accepting the belief as true and then looking for alternatives with positive outcomes. One other way to look for breakthrough is to form links and alliances with external organizations in completely different fields. Come up with a list of alliances you might forge. What would you learn from these organizations, and what could you gain?

Chapter Ten

Driving the Change

What You Can Do to Ensure Your Breakthrough Stays on Course

Many organizations—private, public, and nonprofit—work hard to set up a high-performing, creative culture. They devise programs and processes, build teams, engineer reward systems, and so on. They draft vision statements, embed core values, set horshin and kaizen goals. They hope to make progress. But then the initiative doesn't get underway or goes off course or loses momentum or even alienates staff and managers. This chapter looks at three things: first, the roles that change agents, themselves, can play, or need to have others play, in the change process; second, some reasons why people might resist change or breakthrough; and third, the range of responses staff, volunteers, or even board members might display. We also examine how you might handle those responses.

Roles for Managers and Board Members in Breakthrough

In our experience, breakthrough changes in organizations can't happen without a range of skills and competencies being available to the organization. These skills and competencies can be clustered into roles. These roles can have different names—change agent, change architect, and so on. Managers and board members are often asked to take on these roles. Or they may need to hire outsiders—for example, consultants—to take on the roles.

There are a number of models or typologies to describe the roles that need to be played. We want to introduce you to one we feel is especially suitable for breakthrough situations. The model is one we've developed from an article written for us by the British management consultant Rennie Fritchie (1980). In this article, she argues that in any change process you need people—senior managers, board members, or even external consultants—to behave like the characters in what she calls the "Wild West," using a 1950s cowboy film metaphor. The idea is that change, and particularly breakthrough change, is like the Wild West during the westward expansion period: loaded with huge opportunities and equally huge risks in a relatively unknown and fluid situation.

We've extended and adapted Fritchie's original model, increasing the number of roles from five to seven and changing their emphasis to fit in with our breakthrough emphasis. The seven roles we use are pioneer, wagon train leader, scout, sheriff, homesteader, medicine man or woman, and hired gun. We use these role descriptions and the metaphor when advising on a breakthrough or major change situation. We want to stress that the roles idea is simply a metaphor to help cluster the skills, competencies, knowledge, and qualities needed. The process of change is always more complex than this. But accepting the metaphor, we'll look at each of the roles in more detail.

Pioneer

The pioneer is the person with the vision. This Grizzly Adams-James Fenimore Cooper figure embraces risks and is determined to prove that the apparently impossible is possible—to head west, to reach the ocean, to travel upstream. He or she does the things that everyone else says can't be done.

Pioneers have to be fantastically brave. They must not only have strength of vision and intuition but also be able to deal with hardship, difficulty, and scorn. Not surprisingly, they're often not good team players. Once they've established that the breakthrough *is* possible, they may want—and may need—others to carry it through. People in the organization may need to be very understanding of the pioneer and his or her weird, visionary ways. The pioneer makes it possible for others to make the journey. But he or she may not be good at bringing others along.

Often the visionary initial leader of a nonprofit is the wrong person to take the organization through to maturity. The first CEO of Medicins Sans Frontières (Doctors Without Borders) was such a pioneer. Once the organization was set up, he left. He needed others to make his vision a reality.

Are you a pioneer-in-waiting with an as-yet-unexpressed desire to achieve radical change in your organization? Or do you already have an organizational vision to challenge the status quo and drive toward breakthrough, but need someone else to drive it through? Should you plan to leave once you've sketched out your change idea and set it in motion?

Wagon Train Leader

Your breakthrough may have been sketched out or made believable by a pioneer, but to drive it through you need a wagon train leader. Every wagon train needs a formal leader, aware of the responsibility vested in her, concerned for the overall good, and confident in her ability to complete the journey to a better future. We call this person a wagon trainer. Ideally the wagon trainer is taking a group of people on a trail that she *knows well*. You can trust a wagon trainer to lead you safely because she's done it before—maybe not over this exact terrain, but something pretty similar. What you're getting with this person is *experience*. So a nonprofit may use a CEO, board member, or new staff member to guide it through a change that that person has encountered in a previous position.

The key qualities for a wagon trainer are essentially experience, experience, and experience. She also must be committed to the safety and interests of the group and have the skill to know when to use a scout (described in the next section) to investigate and report on any potential future risks. A wagon trainer will generally take the safest option—the one that minimizes risks. She isn't afraid either to make decisions or to consult whenever necessary. Note that you mustn't confuse wagon trainers and ambitious scouts. If you do decide to appoint a wagon trainer, make sure you're getting real, relevant experience. Typical situations where a nonprofit would need a wagon train leader are when the organization makes the transition from being a national to an international agency or when it launches a major capital or endowment fundraising program. A nonprofit might even use a wagon trainer to integrate a new IT plan.

Several warnings about experience: if your breakthrough is based on an approach others have already used successfully, can you be confident that the breakthrough that worked elsewhere will also work for you? Is yours the same kind of nonprofit or agency? Does the approach still work?

Scout

Every wagon train needs a scout. The scout's job is to go ahead of the main wagon train and identify various opportunities and threats, such as sources of water, robbers, possible floods, difficult terrain, and the like. He then has to report back his findings to the wagon train leader—if possible with a suggested course of action.

Sometimes organizations need a scout to go ahead and find out what's advisable and what is absolutely not. "Ahead" in this sense can mean planning scenarios, creating alternative options, blue sky thinking, or even just analyzing risk. This role is often taken on by an outside consultant because he or she can bring a radical, disinterested view. It can also be taken on by a new CEO or board member who doesn't yet have the baggage of someone long serving but who does have the courage to sketch out possible futures raised by the vision of the pioneer.

The key *qualities* for a scout are to be keen on personal risk taking, to have courage, and to be able to operate alone and not feel isolated. (Scouts are often scouting in situations that are unfamiliar to them.) Unlike the pioneer, however, a scout is working toward a specific goal on behalf of the wagon train. He has to act in the group's interest, and he has a responsibility to share what he finds out in a methodical and useful way. Members of the wagon train have to trust the scout. But remember, scouts can only report back what they've found, or their ideas. It's the wagon train leader who makes the decision or involves the wagon train in making the decision. It's also the wagon trainer who decides between the different ideas of different scouts. It's then up to the wagon train leader or organization to commit to a specific degree of risk. Scouts are often outside consultants. They have expertise in solving certain kinds of challenges. And they enjoy the research or investigation phase, while someone else makes the decision.

Does your change process need you to be a scout who seeks out options? Do you have the qualities to do this or do you need someone else to investigate the risks associated with your change or breakthrough? What risks do you need to assess? Do you know what kind of scout you're looking for? How would you recognize a good scout? How do you plan the future?

Crystal Ball Gazing

In 2000, the U.S.-based Council on Foundations commissioned a scenario-planning exercise looking twenty-five years into the future. It gathered together a number of scouts—consultants, senior CEOs, presidents of foundations, and business leaders. This group went away for a three-day program to discuss likely trends. The result was a set of several possible futures with the implications for foundations and philanthropy worked out. This was really *scientific* crystal ball gazing.

Likewise, at the end of 2000 the Macmillan Cancer Relief charity in the United Kingdom organized a series of "Blue Sky" days with the aim of looking fifteen to twenty years ahead. The organization brought together leading figures in such fields as health care, prevention research, and medical development to explore all the possibilities. But Macmillan consciously advertised for a nonspecialist facilitator to coordinate the events. The charity wanted to have that "outside," disinterested view (very much in keeping with the idea of MBWO—see Chapter Nine).

Sheriff

In the Wild West you often need the benefit of a sheriff. This person is responsible for laying down laws or ground rules for the wagon train once it stops and sets up camp or starts a town. The sheriff defines acceptable and unacceptable behavior. In change processes, individuals can do unusual things to bring all kinds of wild and zany ideas to fruition. They may use crude shortcuts to achieve results. These approaches may work at the time, and maybe they're appropriate in the short term. But after a period of dramatic change, people also need to calm down a little and have some stability and rules and structure. The sheriff's role is to administer "the law"—the necessary systems and structures that stabilize the new situation. He or she will also ensure everyone is treated fairly. The sheriff may have to do a number of things: keep the nonprofit within the law—literally—in terms of things it does; make sure organizational discipline is maintained; and act as a focus for dispute resolution, often in a tough but fair way.

Key qualities for a sheriff are wisdom in applying the rules, a desire to avoid confrontation (but no fear of it if it's necessary), and the understanding that he or she is a law *enforcer*, not a law *maker*. It's worth noting that when the sheriff role and the CEO/chair position are held by one person, that person sometimes confuses his or her will or opinion with the law.

We worked with a homelessness charity that had just lost its wildly charismatic (and disorganized) CEO after five hectic, high-growth years—five years in which the organization had grown hugely, gained credibility, and attracted good people. But this disorganized, unplanned growth was not sustainable. And part of the reason for the resignation of the old CEO was that there were signs of "cracks." The board chose someone dramatically different for the new CEO—a quiet organizer who was tough on systems. The new CEO memorably announced in his opening address to the staff, "I'm not running a hippy commune here," and began over the next few months to really lay down the law in terms of systems and organization, a painful—but essential—process meant to bring stability and structure to the organization and to its work.

Sheriffs are most useful for creating stability. Remember that even in the wildest Wild West towns there had to be some laws and justice. The sheriff role is nearly always an internal one. But it can sit at different levels—with the CEO, his or her deputy, or even a board chair.

Make sure it's clear who is in charge of making the rules and who is in charge of interpreting the rules and making sure things are executed properly. Consider, too, separating these two roles. Too much power is a bad thing. The CEO of our housing nonprofit became quite isolated as he struggled to play sheriff *and* bring people on board. Do you have someone on the board or on your team who acts as sheriff? Is there someone with the mental and organizational toughness to tackle challenges from colleagues? Does this person have wisdom in terms of how to be tough and apply the rules and when to look the other way?

Homesteader

The homesteader is the Jimmy Stewart figure who wants to develop the new community, put down roots, work on developing positive feelings, and create a long-lasting infrastructure. He may not be the most exciting person, but he spots what is helpful for people, and builds on it. This is a key role once a new level of performance has been reached. You should make sure there's a designated homesteader if what's needed is a fulcrum for people to work around or if you want to create enough structural stability and comfort to allow people to try for new performance goals.

Key qualities for a homesteader are a desire for stability, skill in organizing and shaping people's energies, and willingness to play by the new rules and an awareness of how people feel and how to make them feel better. The homesteader is a real team player.

Homesteaders are often underrated in change processes (and may be opposed to the change initially). But you should use them wisely to keep people on board and ensure there are systems and procedures in place to help make any change work. Homesteaders often are from an HR or personnel background. They are concerned about and good at managing the people side of systems. Do you know who in your organization can act as homesteaders? Are they able to identify the key foundations that need to be laid down?

Medicine Man or Woman

Traditional approaches don't always work, and you have to try a bit of magic. (Remember Arthur C. Clarke's famous statement: "Any sufficiently advanced technology is indistinguishable from magic.") The medicine man or woman brings this magic. He or she may be a consultant, a new board member with great fundraising contacts, or a charismatic CEO. Whoever this person is, he or she has a secret weapon: a big idea or a new technique, and it is this that will produce results. For some fundraising nonprofits in the 1990s, it was Ken Burnett and his relationship fundraising. For many organizations now it's the Internet (see the passage "Closing the Digital Divide: The Medicine Woman"). But it could be as simple as a rebranding exercise or a new source of funds. Tony Blair, for example, rebranded the Labour party in the U.K. by calling it the New Labour party and ditching an old-fashioned flag logo for a new-age rose. Within two years, he had won an election by a massive majority as the representative of this party, which had been out of power for seventeen years.

Medicine men and women can inspire people to produce extraordinary results. But they are, of course, fallible, and you need to be sure about them and their idea. The bad news is that the medicine man or woman may be a quack, peddling an idea or solution that doesn't work. For example, reengineering—the big management idea of the 1990s—failed to live up to its promise. And the dot-com revolution proved very bad medicine for many companies. For nonprofits, Internet fundraising never took off. Whatever it is, they have to bring some magic with them to give people confidence that their idea or technique will work. Key qualities for the medicine man or woman are charisma and self-confidence, a "magic bullet," an orientation toward a practical outcome, and the ability to inspire confidence in others. The medicine man or woman can produce extraordinary results. But check out his or her track record. . . . Has the person done this before? Is the magic really revolutionary, or is it an adaptation? How risky is it?

Closing the Digital Divide: The Medicine Woman

Digital Partnerships, a nonprofit in Uttar Pradesh, India, has used the Internet to help close the North-South digital divide. Instead of raising money through the traditional method of selling handicrafts in developed countries made in developing countries, Digital Partnerships makes its income by electronically guarding buildings in New York. The original idea came from a former Swissair employee, Lisa Ros. While at the airline, Ros had observed accounting data being downloaded for processing from terminals all over the world to accountants in India. By the time she returned to work each morning, the data had been uploaded back as full management accounts. (Swissair did this not from a spirit of altruism but because Indian accountants are as highly trained but much cheaper than those in Switzerland.)

In her new job at Digital Partnerships, she felt that the traditional relationship between North and South—based on the South's selling "handicrafts" to the rich North—was fundamentally disempowering. Often the handicrafts produced were not really of interest to Western consumers, couldn't attract a "good" price, and didn't really challenge the skills of the Indian workers making them. The final indignity was that the goods could often be produced cheaper in China, which had even lower labor costs and machinery. Her solution was to think of a way in which she could use the added value of India and Indians in a way that was analogous to the service provided to Swissair.

She came up with a plan to offer twenty-four-hour surveillance of buildings in New York. Surveillance conducted locally in New York City was expensive because of the rates charged by U.S.-based security firms, even when all it involved was someone sitting in a room watching video monitors.

Ros set up the first monitor Internet link using low-cost webcam technology, which connected a New York building and the project in India. Now teams of Indian security staff guard several New York buildings by remote video. If they see anything suspicious, they press an on-screen button. The Internet carries the message back, and that alerts the building owners and the NYPD.

The New York companies pay slightly less for the service, and they get surveillance from people who are fully awake. (Thanks to the time difference, the Indians are working days, not nights.)

In this case, Ros acted as a medicine woman, conjuring up "magic" when it was needed. The result is an economic relationship that crosses the digital divide and brings real benefits to both parties.

Hired Gun

In the Wild West you occasionally need some muscle to do a dirty or difficult job. This is the Clint Eastwood character in every "Man with No Name" spaghetti western. The hired gun is someone engaged specifically to weed out those who don't want to—and won't—sign up to the new breakthrough. For this reason, the hired gun is often an external consultant, someone who can come in, identify key elements to be changed and often the people to be fired or made redundant. They can have no friends.

Their strength is their ability to do—to drive through—a difficult job. Key qualities for the hired gun are clarity of purpose, the ability to work in isolation, and a clear analytic mind. They can, however, have no real friends in the organization. The hired gun may come in for a short period and achieve significant changes. But before asking for the hired gun, you need to have clear answers to these questions: Are these changes really purposeful? What will be left at the end? How will everyone's morale survive?

Now that we've looked more closely at these seven roles, you might like to reflect further on your own situation or organization. Imagine you're in a Wild West movie. What does the "promised

Table 10.1   Wild West Roles: What Do We Need?

Role	Why Do We Need This Role?	Who Can Do It?
Pioneer		
Wagon trainer		
Scout		
Sheriff		
Homesteader		
Medicine man or woman		
Hired gun		

land" look like? How specific and concrete is your vision? How clear and detailed a map do you have of the journey? Is there a well-established route others have taken that you can follow? Where is the unknown territory and what dangers are there in that territory? Who have you consulted about the accuracy of your perception?

Now consider who you need to be with you to make this breakthrough journey. What roles do you need people to play? Are you clear on the skills, qualities, knowledge, and competencies these people need to have? Do you have those people or can you get them from outside? As a way of organizing your thinking on this, you can fill out a chart like the one in Table 10.1.

The Five C's of Change: Why Don't They All Stand Up and Cheer?

So you've got your breakthrough idea, and are clear about the benefits and positive payoffs. You've communicated your vision in a range of ways and to all intelligences. And now you're even clear on the roles you need board members and senior managers to play. But everyone still isn't jumping up and down with excitement about the breakthrough. Why might people be negative toward this approach, which seems so obviously good to you?

They might see the *organizational* consequences as good, but the consequences for them might be bad:

They'll lose their jobs.

They'll lose status and responsibility.

They'll have to relearn lots of skills.

Their existing skills won't be valued or used.

They may not find work as fulfilling.

How can you analyze the type of response you get? And what might you do to bring people on board?

Based on our own research and change work, we've found there are five basic categories of reaction to change that you can watch for and around which you can plan your responses. We call these the five C's of change. To begin to understand these categories, imagine for a moment that you're running a meeting for staff, volunteers, and board members about your breakthrough idea. Figure 10.1 illustrates the approximate distribution curve of the five kinds of responses to the changes proposed at that meeting.

It's important to note that this curve is a snapshot of the distribution at the start of the change process. At any point in this process, a person will be in one category, but he or she can move between categories. Your task is to help as many people as possible on the "basically negative" side of the curve to move over to the "basically positive." To do this you need to understand

Why people are in each category

How you will recognize the response of people in each category

What you need to do to respond to their concerns

Which category you can realistically expect to move them into

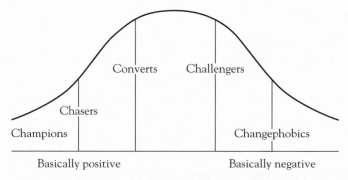

Figure 10.1   Responses to Change: The Five C's

Let's begin by describing how you might recognize the people in each category.

Champions

Champions are usually few in number. They are the ones who are prepared to stick their neck out, run with an idea, and own what happens. They are the people who crowd around you after your presentation on the breakthrough strategy, smiling and shaking your hand. They make up perhaps 5 to 10 percent of the total.

Chasers

Chasers are the people at your presentation who don't immediately respond positively but send you an e-mail later in the day saying they think it's a good idea, having thought about it or discussed it with others. They need a bit of time to reflect and to see who else is on board. At 15 to 20 percent of the total, chasers are a slightly larger group than the champions. Chasers *follow* because they wish to emulate others or because they can, after a pause for reflection, see the advantages of the change. Their less vocal response following your presentation may leave you feeling worried that they are not as excited by the new strategy as you hoped. (And, in truth, they probably aren't.) But you need to keep your nerve with chasers.

Converts

Converts listen in silence to your presentation and tend to say little even when you ask for questions. They are the biggest single group at 30 to 40 percent. They are not particularly vocal for or against, but you probably find their silence quite intimidating and unnerving, and you can confuse the silence with negativity. Converts are likely to require solid evidence in favor of the change in order to come on board. They need to be convinced that you've thought through your proposal, and they need solid reassurance about what impact the changes will have on *them*. You may leave the presentation worried that these people aren't really excited by or on board with your strategy. (And, in truth, they probably aren't.)

Challengers

Challengers will ask difficult questions initially and then . . . continue to do so. Their basic approach to things is to confront and to be awkward. They generally resist or challenge the change, not because they are of evil intent but because they care or have a strong stake in the outcome. They are operating from the "If it ain't broke . . ." stance, so they'll use a very fine net indeed to trawl for flaws and drawbacks in your plan. And they're not afraid to tell you their concerns, no matter who you are. If these people can be convinced that the breakthrough strategy is necessary to close down their opposition, the strategy will succeed. If you *don't* win them over or at least persuade them to stop criticizing, however, they will continue to cause problems and even discontent. This group makes up 15 to 20 percent of the total, so you may feel that you're getting a lot of negative feedback at your hypothetical meeting.

Changephobics

No matter how irrational their fears are, changephobics will not be convinced. They are generally few in number—5 to 10 percent—

but are still important insofar as they can slow down or—in extreme circumstances—even derail change. They may not be vocal, at least not directly, but they will cause dissent or stir things up. And they are essentially immovable. This last characteristic is important, as it will have an impact on your proposed breakthrough. Changephobics are tough.

How to Respond to the Five C's

As the change agent, you will need to tailor your approach to each of the five C's.

Champions

Often change agents like the idea of champions; after all, these are the ones who immediately congratulate you on your acumen for introducing this breakthrough strategy. But you need to treat champions cautiously. They have advantages, no question: they support you, act as advocates with other people, and will carry out your commands unswervingly.

But they have disadvantages too. For one thing, they are generally champions of *everything*. They might be similarly enthusiastic about your proposal to paint the office green. This tendency *can* make them poor judges of what makes something fly, and they may give you a false impression of how well your proposal has gone down overall. As a result of the aforementioned tendency, champions' endorsement may not be very highly regarded by other members of staff. In fact, their endorsement may work against you. (Think of Toad in *Wind in the Willows*, who always wanted the latest thing.) Another disadvantage is that they will not question you closely on your idea or its merits and so may blindly follow your ideas without really thinking them through. This can be dangerous, for you *and* for them. You need some challenge to ensure your idea has some rigor.

How should you deal with champions? Give them something practical to do, which absorbs their energy. Be careful about using them as advocates for what you want to achieve. They may be treated with a lot of caution or skepticism by others.

Chasers

Chasers are the ones who, at the end of a briefing meeting, will be looking around to see who else is on board. They will discuss your proposal with others before forming a judgment and will generally look to a key opinion maker or "trigger" person for guidance. They, too, have their advantages: they give you a more accurate view of how your idea is going down. Their joining in is a sign that you're making progress, and, once committed, they will stay with you.

Of course there are some disadvantages associated with them as well. They will come on board only if you convince the right trigger person, and they will not come on board *immediately*. That pause or gap may leave you feeling anxious (and leave others wondering if you're going to succeed). Further, they may need reassurance about a concern very specific to them. For example, suppose there is to be a restructuring coming out of the breakthrough strategy you are proposing. The chasers may be anxious about the specific impact of that restructuring on their team.

To bring chasers on board, you need to identify key influencers or trigger people at various levels. Brief them in advance, and they'll encourage the chasers. (Think of organizing a party when you were at school. Once you'd identified the most popular person in your class and persuaded him or her to come to the party, everyone else agreed to turn up.)

Converts

There are two general advantages to this group. One is that because they usually form the majority of the group, your succeeding at bringing them on board ensures that your idea or breakthrough will be adopted. The other is that although they tend to be slow to *adopt* a change or innovation, they are equally slow to let it go. You have *momentum* once they're on board.

Converts too have their disadvantages. They may take so long to come on board that an opportunity you wanted to seize is lost. You may find that your initiative loses momentum or focus, especially if you end up responding to a whole range of small issues that concern them.

Think carefully about converts' concerns before launching your initiative. If you can address them in advance, you'll be able to bring this group on board more quickly. You may find that preparing and presenting a list of what you believe will be issues of concern as FAQs helps. The presentation of this list says to your staff that you've thought about their needs and interests.

Why Are People Motivated to Oppose Your Change?

People in your organization may resist change for all sorts of reasons, including the following:

Organizational history: past resentments, unhappy experiences, broken or unfulfilled promises, shifting alliances

Organizational relationships: perceived imbalances in power and authority, trust levels between staff and managers, communication channels and how effective they are

Personal uncertainties: self-perception of status or loss of status, competence concerns, level of security, own development interests, loss of power

Lack of information: people not knowing what to do or why they have to do something

Be clear about what is *motivating* people's resistance. Certain factors may be easier to work on than others—for example, lack of information is easier to correct than lack of trust.

Challengers

The challengers want to test out your ideas to the limit and, as you might expect, ask difficult questions. They need careful handling.

There are advantages to having challengers to contend with, even though they may not seem immediately apparent: their difficult questions *force* you to be thorough about examining your thinking or plan. And, because they may well ask these questions on behalf of others, especially the converts, dealing with them may enable you indirectly to reassure those others.

It is no surprise that there are some disadvantages to challengers as well. They can carry on asking difficult questions beyond the point at which doing so is useful. They also may ask questions on issues that you regard as inappropriate or that you think are too sensitive or not up for discussion. In all these situations, you need to be clear with them about where the boundaries are.

When dealing with challengers it's important that you handle their queries fairly, however irritated you may feel. Others are watching. You also need to be firm with them about what's "off the agenda." For example, you might say, "We *can* discuss the way we reorganize and the total investment expenditure; we *won't* discuss the fact that we're going to have a reorganization by December and that other budgets will have to be cut to pay for the new project." And you need to stick to these ground rules.

Changephobics

Changephobics are difficult. They will oppose your idea on principle. They have no direct advantages, because from your perspective, they are intractably opposed to your idea or scheme. The only advantage to having them around is that if you are seen as capable of dealing with them honestly and fairly, you will gain brownie points from others who'll perceive you as just and evenhanded. Consigning people to the category of changephobic is serious. To label someone a changephobic means you believe they will *always* oppose your approach. Do it only after careful consideration. They don't oppose your proposal because they're bad people, of course, but rather because they feel you're destroying something they value or directly attacking them or their situation.

The disadvantages of changephobics are legion. Among them: they will do their best to stop your initiative, they will always be opposed to it, and they can significantly lower morale among others.

The harsh reality is that you *have* to get rid of changephobics as quickly and effectively as you can. You may want to move them to another section or department, or you may need to ask them to leave.

Dealing with Changephobics: There's Always Another Point of View

Several years ago, we were running a change and innovation program for the British Red Cross, which involved significant change in role and status for those managers involved. We used the five C's with a group of managers and expressed the view that "of course, no one here is a changephobic" (though we knew a number were). Up stood an older man, one of the group whose job titles and status were under threat. "I am completely opposed to these proposals. And as a result of that you may regard me as a changephobic," he said. He paused as he tried to control his evidently strong feelings. "But let me tell you, after twenty-five years of service to the Red Cross, I feel like a different C. I feel like a *casualty*." The room chilled, and we froze as we realized how much our categories were dependent on *our perspective*. We understood that while he was absolutely a changephobic and opposed to the proposals, we had a responsibility to be respectful of his principled opposition. Ironically, it was part of our job to make absolutely sure he left, but it also was important that he left with dignity. This approach was important for us, for him, and also for the other managers involved in the change.

Summary

When you set up your change process, you will need access to certain skills, knowledge, competencies, and qualities. You may need to think about which role or roles fit these skills, knowledge, competencies, and qualities and how competent you or others in your organization are to play them. If you don't find someone inside your organization to play the roles, go outside to find them.

We tend to emphasize the *benefits to the organization* when planning breakthrough change. But not everyone judges the impact of things through organizational perspectives or, for that matter, even values future benefits. Even when you have your Wild West team in place, you still need to reflect on how individuals in the organization will react or respond to your change announcement. The responses you receive can be thought of as falling into five categories: the five C's. Each of the C's comes out of a different motivation, each has different and sometimes surprising pluses and minuses, and each requires a different approach from you.

Action

Think about your breakthrough change as a movie script. Who is in the cast? What's the story of your journey? What does that promised land look like? How will you recognize when you're there? Are you clear? Can you make it real for others? How will people feel when they get there? Relieved? Excited? Or what? Who's writing the script? Is it finished or in draft?

Make a list of what roles you need in your change processes and who can play them. If you don't have anyone on the team or the board who can fill these roles, can you hire them in? What skills, knowledge, competencies, and qualities do you need?

Think about the stakeholders in your organization: staff, volunteers, board, and even users. Which of the C's would they fit in if you announced your breakthrough now? If you had them all in one room, what would you need to do with each of the C's?

- What can you get the *champions* to do so that they feel positive but don't block your view of reality?
- Who do you need to convince to get the *chasers* on board? Who are the opinion makers in your organization?

- What questions do you need to ask and answer on behalf of the *converts?* What reassurance do they need?

- Who are the *challengers?* What flaws might they spot in your argument? How can you anticipate these flaws? Which parts of your proposal are open to challenge and which parts are not?

- Who are the *changephobics?* How can you help them go or get them to leave? How can you ensure that you've been seen to behave properly towards them?

Chapter Eleven

Working in the Breakthrough Organization

How to Change the Way You Work to Prepare for Breakthrough

The *way* people work can have a significant impact on your organization's readiness to accept or adopt a breakthrough. This chapter looks at three aspects of working life that can help build or sustain a breakthrough culture:

- How symbols, especially *job titles*, can affect the roles people play and change their perceptions of how they might be able to improve performance
- How the *physical workspace* is organized to promote various kinds of interaction and connection between individuals and teams
- How *multiple intelligences* can be switched on in the workplace in order to provoke new ways of thinking and acting

Simply making changes in these areas won't magically create a breakthrough organization, of course, but it will signal to others that you want to create a framework in which breakthrough is possible. And some changes will help bring about an environment in which creativity and innovation are more easily nurtured.

Changing Focus, Changing Job Titles

The symbolic aspects of an organization can be vital, for they are a strong indication of culture—and culture can impact strongly on organizational performance. The days of executive washrooms may be gone, but there are new "distinctions": Who has his palm pilot paid for? Who can decide without authorization to work at home? Who travels business class?

Names are important symbols, too. For example, if your organization, like so many others, is made up of *divisions*—the program division, the fundraising division, the marketing division—is it any surprise that the various divisions don't get along? We've often also wondered why key board meetings to discuss the way forward privately are called "retreats."

One sign of a creative organization challenging its old ways of thinking is the adoption of different or even "weird" job titles. Some job title changes are just cosmetic, but some, especially those that permeate the whole organization, represent a significant shift in the way staff and managers are meant to think and act. At its simplest level, a new title signals a brand-new role. For example, increasingly, organizations are appointing a chief knowledge officer, a role that is becoming as important as that of chief financial officer. The latter manages one kind of resource (money), the former an equally important but less tangible resource, information and knowledge. (These new job titles, common in Internet and high-tech companies, are starting to seep into nonprofits, although the strongest examples are still in the private sector.)

Some changes in job titles are meant to signal a change in role or focus for a staff member. Bill Gates recently announced that he would no longer be known as chairman of Microsoft, but rather as chief software architect, reflecting his desire to be more involved in practical projects. And Steve Jobs, Gates's opponent in most things, has opted for iCEO (Internet chief executive officer), to signal how important the Internet is to the future of Apple. Ben and Jerry's has a primal ice cream therapist, whose job it is to maintain the company's reputation for unusual combinations of flavors. The CEO of Joe Boxer has an alternative title of chief underpants officer, emphasizing the company's core business. These title changes are not, we believe, just for fun. They represent a way to help colleagues and customers understand the role these senior people will play.

The best place to find out what's hot is the "Job Titles of the

Future" column in *Fast Company* magazine. (You also can visit a searchable website at FastCompany.com.) This column highlights new organizational titles and responsibilities and gives little biographies of the postholders and their duties. Some of the titles featured in the magazine recently have included *minister of order and reason, princess of persuasion, keeper of the magic, vibe evolver,* and *asset appraiser.* All of these are real jobs for real people, an outward sign of organizations' trying to think in new ways about the way they work. (The princess of persuasion is a PR officer to you and me.)

This move away from traditional job titles picks up on a number of trends:

> There is an uncertainty about hierarchy and structure that makes some titles obsolete or irrelevant.
>
> Newer, younger people—including CEOs—may prefer a more relaxed, funky style, from their weird company job title to the Nike trainers they wear at work as part of a dress-down-every-day approach.
>
> As indicated earlier, new jobs may need new titles. For example, there was no call for a webmaster before the Web existed. On the other hand, some of these titles are ways to describe traditional work carried out in a new way. For example, Oxfam, the leading U.K. relief agency, had to create the position of emergency accountant. The job is to arrive in a disaster situation, such as Somalia during the famine, and manage the large amount of cash needed to pay for local services without the receipts or invoices that conventional accountants so prize.

An article by Peter Freedman in the United Kingdom's *Sunday Times* (2000) noted some interesting European examples of title changes and the rationales for these changes. Kenny Hirschhorn is director of strategy, imagineering and futurology at Orange, a fast-expanding mobile phone company. He argues that his unusual job title puzzles and interests people to whom he gives his business card.

In that way, he has a chance to explain his different philosophy of doing business. Hirschhorn is insistent that his approach is carried out across the entire company. He ensures that other employees of Orange have "different" titles, including ambassador of strategy, knowledge consultant, and techneurologist.

The same article mentions a British marketing consultancy, The Forth Room, which has also made changes across all levels of staff:

Old Title	New Title
CEO	Pacemaker
Senior consultant	Pathfinder
Analyst	Sleuth
Public relations	Attention seeker
Receptionist	Welcomer

What's the purpose of this renaming activity? There are several, says the CEO—sorry, pacemaker—at The Forth Room, including that it can help your organization differentiate itself and can focus the mind of the title owner on what his or her real job is.

Fast Company gives another example (Dykson, 1999). The Chicago law firm Schiff, Hardin, and Waite has gone further than any other firm in what is normally a deeply conservative industry. A company of almost 250 lawyers, 150 years old, has a Department of Fun, which has within it a manager of mischief and a creator of celebrations. The manager of mischief's responsibilities include helping the staff—including lawyers—relax. He also sends rhyming e-mails. On their website, they're keen to stress that they see such roles as being part of maintaining a work-life balance in an industry that can demand long and punishing hours.

Reflect for a moment on your own job title and how accurately it reflects what you do or, indeed, what you should do. Think about how you could change your job title so as to reflect your actual role, perhaps a radically different role as your organization changes to meet new challenges. Consider, too, the difference between your *internal and external* roles and your current role and the role you hope for in the future. Could you have two job titles? For example, your *formal* title might be chief financial officer, but would it be more accurate and specific to describe you as manager of the money flow, guardian of the purse, or keeper of financial ethics?

U.S. Foundations' CEOs Change Titles

At the Conference on Community Foundations in September 2000, almost three hundred CEOs and presidents of America's largest community foundations—representing $7 billion dedicated to philanthropy—agreed to tear up their business cards and make new ones describing their role more accurately. For despite the fact that they all had the title *president* or *CEO* on their cards, they performed radically different functions in their organizations: stimulator, visionary, and stabilizer, among others. Although most felt they fulfilled several roles, they were encouraged to define the one that was overarching.

Rose Meissner, president of the St. Joseph's Foundation in Indiana, gave herself the title of *believer.* She said that this title described the role she played in the foundation: someone who encouraged others to take risks and maintained support in difficult times. Dot Wheeler, president of the community foundation network, restyled her job title as *chief conciliator,* more accurately reflecting her role as someone who had to maintain a balance between the different forces within the network. (Community foundations are locally based, fundraising organizations based in specific localities. They are members of the Council on Foundations and meet once a year for a major conference.)

Change the Space, Change the Minds, Change the Way People Work

Changing job titles is almost certainly not enough to change the culture of your organization. The ideal *place* to work is a genuinely engaging workspace—a place where the very structure, décor, and layout of the building encourages people to think in a creative and innovative way.

So what would an engaging workplace be like? It would actually set out to provide emotional and sensory enrichment by the way it was laid out, the building materials used, and the interactions it promoted.

An emotionally enriched environment is one where people feel physically relaxed but mentally switched on. Think for a moment: How often have you cracked a work problem while relaxing on vacation? Take away the stressors or the tension, and your mind is freed to think creatively and laterally. How can you create that kind of atmosphere in your workplace?

A second issue to consider is that of sensory enrichment: increasing people's awareness of their environment and making sure they are energized by it. Striving for *emotional* enrichment, some organizations spend a lot of money on the classic motivational posters. (You know the ones we mean—with mountains and eagles and rowing teams and slogans.) These *can* work at one level by providing visual stimulation, but, of course, after a couple of weeks people stop noticing them because they've become part of the background. You need to constantly change the sensory stimulus.

Emotional and sensory enrichment are important. But the single biggest element in culture change is workspace layout. Layout can have a huge impact on the kind of creativity and innovation an organization can generate, and even on how well it operates generally.

Before you plan to change or organize a workspace, you need to be clear about what you want to use it for—its purpose. You then work back from there to create the right stimulus in terms of sensory and emotional enrichment as well as the right structure for the purpose. We'll deal more with sensory or emotional enrichment in the next section, "Using Multiple Intelligences in the Workplace." Here, we'll deal specifically with structure.

The purpose (or purposes) of your workspace can be as diverse as

- To promote a certain kind of *planned* communication
- To encourage *unplanned and informal* communication
- To generate a sense of team feeling and shared work
- To allow different sections to work together on certain activities
- To enable people to work by themselves on individual projects
- To allow spaces for quiet reflection and spaces for lively discussion

How you go about ensuring that the workspace fulfills that purpose can vary. Some issues to consider when you're trying to reorganize a workspace around a purpose are:

- The way the space is laid out—open plan or individual offices
- The allocation of common spaces to specific activities versus having multi-use spaces.
- The extent to which staff members themselves can plan any changes and allocations
- The way in which fixed mood-influencing elements—color, furniture, fabric, lighting, and so on—are used

There isn't a right answer to these issues. But there are lots of good examples of organizations thinking about their spaces. (Have a look at your office. Is it full of gray office equipment and evenly lit by fluorescents?)

How Organizations Use Their Space to Create Culture and Creativity

The Idea Factory in San Francisco produces some radical ideas and uses its space to help create them. The company has a single, hanger-like building split up in a number of ways: there's a theatre complete with moveable benches and a lighting rig to encourage action or rehearsal; there's a screened-off cubicle to use computers and have productive left brain time; there's a library with racks of books, made to feel like a quiet reflective space; there's a space with dollhouse-size equipment and small plastic figures to encourage creative role plays and scenarios; there's a meeting room without real walls—instead there are tilted designers' tables covered with paper for sketching and writing to encourage the outflow of ideas.

The purpose of this rich working environment is to enable the Idea Factory's customers and staff to create directly any experience they want so as to "rehearse" future projects or identify problems in existing systems. The dominant metaphor is of a Hollywood studio—you can make it what you want.

The award-winning advertising agency St. Luke's does a lot of work with nonprofits. It has come from nowhere to be the most successful agency in the United Kingdom in less than five years. Part of the reason for the agency's success is that it creates workspaces for its teams modeled on its clients' own spaces. For a railway company account, for example, St. Luke's created an office space like a railway carriage so that the team could really get into the brief when they discussed the client.

The Design Council in London is one of the leading European nonprofits responsible for promoting good design. Its offices are completely open plan, and the CEO sits at one large desk with all his colleagues. The idea is to engender a spirit of teamwork and openness across the organization.

Go to see the offices of Greenpeace in London and you can imagine you are in a giant sailing ship. Hung from the ceiling are great "sails" made of cloth. These are designed both to quiet the minds at work in this frenetic organization and to exemplify the wind-power principles key to Greenpeace's philosophy.

Visit the Millbank headquarters of the British Labour Party, which transformed itself and swept to power in 1997, after seventeen years in opposition. On one floor are all the managers and their various teams spread out in a spider's web pattern. At the center sit the key political coordinators. The purpose is to create "waves" as ideas, campaigns, and challenges reverberate around the room.

If you ever visit Stockholm, you should try to take in The Future Center of Skandia, a special R&D center concerned with breakthrough products. The vice president of intellectual capital, Leif Edvinsson, has introduced a number of ways to stimulate the senses and thus, he believes, creativity:

- As you enter from outside you are calmed by the sounds of ocean waves.
- Inside there is classical music to stimulate the right brain.
- The second floor has the smell of baking bread wafted in to create a relaxed, homey feel.

You may not agree that Edvinsson has found the right stimuli, but he's working in a coherent planned way to manage his staff's environment.

Finally, you can think about how to organize people according to the kind of work they need to do. What follows is a simple typology that we've adapted from a book by Francis Duffy (1997). Duffy points out that the move is away from what he calls hives—lots of workers operating in open-plan space and overseen—and toward balancing the opportunities for interaction and autonomy. There are three main ways to do this:

Dens: these are suitable for work where high interaction and low autonomy are needed. These clusters of desks are good for short-term, intense cooperative work, such as organizing a special event.

Cells: these individual spaces—separate offices or "Dilbert"- like cubicles—are suitable for individuals working in concentrated, short, uninterrupted bursts. People may go out to work elsewhere temporarily and then come back to their cell, and they want it left as it was. You probably need cells for writing and quiet planning.

Clubs: this is space that people can move into to work together. They should also be able to move out from the club to work on individual projects to gain the autonomy they need. This is very suitable for campaigns or for specific projects.

You might like to conduct an audit of your current spaces against the kind of work you want to promote. How many dens, cells, and clubs do you need?

Just as you can develop your own personal, multiple intelligences (see Chapter Five), you can move on to work on the general idea of a fully intelligent workspace. This is a workspace and a work style that tries to *switch on* specific intelligences by managing the environment, the way activities are carried out, or the communications techniques used. Stimulating the different intelligences will undoubtedly help you develop or sell your breakthrough idea across the organization. It will help you communicate effectively with an individual or a team that has a particular strength in one intelligence and choose the appropriate leadership or management style to use in order to "sign up" people to the breakthrough. Finally, it will actually encourage individuals and groups to connect to or challenge each other, so increasing overall potential for breakthrough.

World Bank Scores Own Goal?

James Wolfensohn, president of the World Bank, is not a man well known for his multiple intelligences in an organization notorious for its commitment to logical/mathematical intelligence, whatever the human cost. But he and the organization are trying to improve.

In 1999 Wolfensohn began a teamwork program. As part of it he drew on a soccer team metaphor. A small goal was set up in the foyer of the bank in Washington. Senior executives were asked to line up and kick soccer balls into the net, demonstrating their commitment to score better this year as a team. More than that, senior staff were told to wear little ball-shaped lapel badges to remind them that they're on the same team.

Wolfensohn's approach may not be perfect, but it's an attempt to demonstrate the kinesthetic and emotional kinds of intelligence the bank lacked in the past.

So those are the benefits. How do you create this fully intelligent workspace? We've already seen that there are at least seven distinct intelligences:

1. Logical/mathematical
2. Creative/musical
3. Linguistic
4. Spatial/visual
5. Physical/kinesthetic
6. Emotional/interpersonal
7. Intrapersonal

You can switch on these intelligences in various ways in the workplace. Here are some ideas for each of the seven.

• *Switching on logical/mathematical intelligence.* You're probably most used to using logical/mathematical intelligence at work anyway. Any time you find yourself prioritizing, sorting, reasoning, sequencing, evaluating, or assessing, you're using it.

If you want to warm up your team for this kind of activity, try giving them quizzes, puzzles, case studies, and budget-based challenges. And if you want them to *focus* on this intelligence, give them computers, pads, pencils, paper, and other such materials. Ask them to produce business cases, project plans, and cost-benefit analyses.

- *Switching on creative/musical intelligence.* This is perhaps the hardest intelligence to use effectively in the workplace, partly because one person's musical passion may be another's nightmare. But you *can* use music and rhyme to affect performance. IBM used to have a company song with which it opened sales conferences. Mazda commissioned Michael Nyman to write them a company tune to be played in public spaces in their workplaces. The New Zealand rugby team, the All Blacks, use a "haka" or Maori war chant to get themselves pumped up for the big game. One of the United Kingdom's largest nonprofits, the Women's Institute, opens and closes all its meetings with an inspirational William Blake poem, "Jerusalem," set to music.

Think even about rhyme as a kind of musical-tonal stimulus that makes such slogans as FedEx's "Absolutely, positively, on time, every time" a kind of music. How could you make your overlong and rambling mission statement into a snappy rap or a memorable slogan? Or is there a piece of music that might inspire people to think in new ways?

- *Switching on linguistic intelligence.* Linguistic intelligence is more likely to be switched on if you can find a way to get people to speak and put things in their own words. This might mean encouraging them to write materials or write down ideas and share them. Or it could mean setting up a formal debate on a breakthrough idea—with one side for and the other side against the idea.

It's good to have a well-crafted and detailed organizational vision or mission statement. It's better if people also have their own quick-and-dirty version of it. Again, there are some excellent commercial examples. Coca-Cola has a great and sweeping mission statement full of vision and values. But its one-liner is, "Never more than an arm's length from a Coca-Cola." And remember Avis's famous "We try harder"? In the nonprofit world, Amnesty International has a one-liner, "Remembering the forgotten victim." And UNICEF uses, "A world where no child goes to bed hungry." What's yours? And if you haven't got a quick-and-dirty one-liner, could you get one?

- *Switching on spatial/visual intelligence.* This is perhaps the easiest intelligence to switch on—mindmaps, Post-its, flipcharts, whiteboards, and the like can all help. Anything that involves changing the usual space—posters, banners, and slogans. Remember, though, don't leave anything up for too long in the same space or it will become "wallpaper." Visualizing and imaging things is good in this context. We've run a guided fantasy for three hundred fundraisers, asking them to see themselves achieving their targets two years in the future. We got them all to shut their eyes and imagine switching on their computers. "Imagine," we said, "you can now see your fundraising target as an Excel spreadsheet. Notice that you're at 110 percent of target."

• *Switching on physical/kinesthetic intelligence.* Sometimes in a workplace meeting you can see people fidgeting and looking restless. They may be bored, or they may need some stimulation of their physical/kinesthetic intelligence.

To switch on physical/kinesthetic intelligence, get them up, moving around, and handling things. If you want them to be excited about your vision of a new building, make up a model and get them to walk around it and touch it. Give them samples of some of the fabrics: material swatches for chair coverings and carpet samples that they can walk on. Take them to see similar buildings to get a sense of what they'd like. If you want to run a kinesthetic brainstorming meeting, don't have everyone seated shouting out ideas for you to write on a flipchart. Instead, give everyone a pack of Post-its and a pen. Get them to write down ideas and stick them up on a wall.

Using Multiple Intelligences in Fundraising

There are lots of opportunities to use multiple intelligences in a practical setting, as in the following example. At the University of Monterrey in Mexico, the two talented fundraisers, Isabella Navarro Grueter and Adalberto Viesca, have achieved extraordinary results in a country still relatively new to fundraising. Their "Appeal to Values" has raised $25 million in just three years. This is a huge sum in

Mexico—easily three times the previous highest target achieved by an academic institution.

Part of their success lies in the fact that they've created a fabulous fundraising environment, rich in the use of multiple intelligences:

- An elaborate and carefully worded case statement emphasizing the importance of the university work (linguistic and emotional).
- A snappy, one-line slogan, "Appeal to Values" (linguistic). (It sounds better in Spanish!)
- A range of fulfillment gifts for donors, including some beautiful craft objects (kinesthetic and visual).
- Specially designed and engineered bricks that make up a walkway connecting different parts of the campus. Each of these bricks is a memento of a donor gift. Prospective donors are taken on a tour along the walkway to read the statements other donors have written on their bricks (kinesthetic, spatial/visual, and linguistic).
- A large and prominent bell on a raised area that is rung to symbolize any major fundraising successes (kinesthetic and musical). (This same bell also is rung at graduation ceremonies, so it has a stirring impact on alumni.)

- *Switching on emotional/interpersonal intelligence*. Interpersonal intelligence is often referred to as "thinking with the mouth open." This involves promoting discussion, openness, listening, and exchanging views in a friendly and sociable way. These exchanges needn't take place in a formal setting—an office kitchen or water cooler can prove ideal for interpersonal intelligence. (Think of the bathroom in *Ally McBeal*.)

Social events like picnics, trips to the bowling alley, and barbecues can also nurture interpersonal intelligence, especially if they involve finding out more about other people in a nonwork setting. We need to regard these kinds of activities as not just fun; they do actually have a specific purpose.

• *Switching on intrapersonal intelligence.* Intrapersonal intelligence is "thinking with the mouth closed," which results in considered and balanced views. It can be switched on by encouraging more individual reflection and considered thought. It's complementary to interpersonal intelligence.

Sometimes it's tempting to jump to early solutions or conclusions if people speak unformed thoughts too soon. By stimulating intrapersonal intelligence, you can encourage individuals to think more before speaking. Why not try to begin each meeting about your breakthrough with a moment's quiet reflection? Why not get people to write down their opinions and then reflect on them *before* the meeting? Do you have a space in your work setting devoted to quiet thought—no phones, no computers, no fax machines, no talking, just quiet thought?

You can also extend intrapersonal intelligence to encompass your ethics and values. Does your organization have a clear code of ethics and values that it lives by? Are these displayed prominently? Are copies given to individuals to take away and reflect on? All World Wide Fund (WWF) employees carry a business card made from recycled paper, with a copy of the WWF value statement printed on its back. This is partly for employees, but it also encourages recipients of the card to consider these values.

A Mexican recycling project, Hechos Deshechos, chooses to demonstrate its values in a very physical way. Each employee has to wear an obvious item of clothing made from recycled materials. For example, the CEO, Manuel des Rios, wears a tie that is actually made from recycled beer cans. It both reminds *him* of the organization's mission and values and demonstrates to others that he and the other employees of Hechos Deshechos mean what they say.

Summary

Your breakthrough needs an environment where it's *actively* encouraged and developed. It also needs an environment in which it is maintained and, if appropriate, challenged. You can do this in a range of ways, some symbolic, some practical:

- By changing or adapting job titles to reflect what people actually do or should do. This also can help when dealing with outside customers or users.
- By physically changing your space to make an impact on how individuals and teams act and interact. You should begin with the kinds of action and interaction you want and then design or create the space.
- By creating an environment that stimulates or switches on all the intelligences. This is especially important for creating a really rich and fulfilling workspace.

Action

Perhaps the best place to begin is with yourself:

- Take out your business card, cross out your job title, and write down what your real *role* is in your organization. Do other people know what you do? How could you rename your colleagues' jobs?
- Consider what kind of work people need to do in your office. How suitable is the layout for doing that work effectively? What could you do to change it? Could you create spaces for different kinds of work—clubs, cells, or dens? Do people have the tools they need—whiteboards, flipcharts, soft chairs?
- Look around your own office. How many intelligences does your office switch on? How many does it miss? Do the colors, fabrics, lighting, and textures in your office create the right atmosphere? Could you alter that atmosphere with flowers, cookies, real coffee, music?

Conclusion

Confession time. This isn't the book we set out to write. We *wanted* to write—and you might have wanted to buy—a slim little volume called something like *Five Easy Steps to Breakthrough Thinking*. Hah! If only.

The challenge was that the more we tried to pin down a simple, seductive formula, the clearer it became that the reality was just a whole lot messier and more complex. So we opted, as you've found, for a toolbox: a collection of approaches and ideas that, used appropriately, can create a composite whole from disparate parts. Remember, too, that in a toolbox some tools are easy to use, some require skill and practice. Be prepared to put in that practice, and the techniques will work as well for you as they have for others.

But we don't want to completely disappoint you. Less in the spirit of today's culture of speedy gratification and more in the spirit of summary, we propose to leave you with the five key principles we believe you need to achieve breakthrough.

1. *Have a vision.* Make it an unreasonable and demanding one. Accept neither compromise nor dilution: they are the enemies of breakthrough. Avoid the tyranny of incrementalism. Dream of unlocking your own and your organization's potential.

2. *Set an urgent and demanding time frame.* "Urgent and demanding" can often appear to be ridiculous. But depending on the challenge, it can mean achieving the vision next week or

focusing on it for the next ten years. Whatever, set a time. And create overwhelming urgency and momentum about achieving the result you need. Use this urgency and momentum to unlock creativity.

3. *Share your vision.* Invent words, phrases, and themes to share your idea widely. Look for weird, bizarre ways to do it. Appeal to every intelligence. Use stories, metaphors, and parables. Avoid, at all costs, the brushed aluminum vision plaque on the wall. Be aware of the new and possibly uncomfortable roles you might have to play to achieve the result. Be aware, too, of how different people will respond to the vision (remember the 5C's).

4. *Avoid limiting beliefs.* Watch out for mind-sets—your own or others'—that reduce your vision or undermine your belief in the possible.

5. *Look for inspiration everywhere.* The greatest inspiration comes from the oddest places. Be open to it. Look for inspiration in the newspapers, in your local coffee shop, in art galleries. Avoid management books. . . . Be aware of how your brain works, and seek to work with both sides of your brain.

We said at the start that we regard this book as work in progress. We'd love to hear back from you about your experience in your own organization or about other organizations you know of that are breaking new ground. And we'd love to share some of these ideas and practices in workshop form with you. You can get in touch with us by e-mail at tmc@managementcentre.co.uk.

=mc is an international management consultancy and management training organization that works to transform the work of nonprofits worldwide. To find out more about us or our work, visit www.managementcentre.co.uk.

Select Breakthrough Thinking Booklist

This booklist is designed to help you extend and stretch your thinking on the topics raised in the book.

Change and Strategy

Disorganisation: The Handbook of Organisational Strategy
Brian Clegg and Paul Birch
FT/Pitman, London, 1998
ISBN: 0-2736-3107-1
This is an imaginative book on how to manage disorganization. It includes a useful summary of the Insight Jungian model to assess how different people can make different contributions to change. It contains a number of useful case studies on how organizations are trying to become less rigid.

Organisational Change
Barbara Senior
Pitman, London, 1997
ISBN: 0-2736-2491-1
A really good "big picture" overview of the change process from the point of view of the whole organization. It contains a number of useful analysis models and a very useful discussion on how structure impacts an organizational culture.

Five Frogs on a Log
Mark Feldman and Michael Spratt
Wiley, London, 1999
ISBN: 0-4719-8823-5
A stimulating book on the ways in which the corporate world is trying to change to take account of the new change drivers. It's full of nice examples of paradigm shifts in thinking.

Funky Business
K. Nordstrom and J. Ridderstale
FT.com, London, 2000
ISBN: 0-2736-4591-9
This book explores how funkiness has become the new cultural necessity for the adaptive and successful corporation. Good examples and case studies, especially about how knowledge management impacts on organizations.

Smart Things to Know About Strategy
Richard Koch
Capstone, Oxford, 2000
ISBN: 1- 8411-2034-0
A quick, smart, and snappy guide to strategy and strategic thinking and how it has changed over the last twenty to thirty years. Very good on the limitations of predicting change and innovation.

Creativity and Innovation

Creativity for Managers
Alan Barker
The Industrial Society, London, 1995
ISBN: 1-8583-5148-0
This book has a good list of how-to ideas on the subject of creativity and, interestingly, has a Jungian spin on the psychology of the topic. A practical guide rather than a source of examples.

How to Get Ideas
Jack Foster
Berrett-Koehler, San Francisco 1996
ISBN: 1-5677-5006-X
This is a really fun and stimulating book—mostly using advertising examples, but still valuable on the subject of how to stimulate pure creativity. Some useful techniques for brainstorming are explained.

Serious Creativity
Edward de Bono
HarperCollins Business, London, 1995
ISBN: 0-0063-7958-3
A well-written and comprehensive book on the whole issue of applied creativity, written by the guru on the subject. Lots of examples of tools and techniques.

When Sparks Fly
Dorothy Leonard and Walter Swap
Harvard Business Press, Harvard, 1999
ISBN: 0-8758-4865-6
This is an excellent book full of case studies and anecdotes on how businesses make organizations and teams become more creative. Brings real scholarly insight into what creativity is and how it can be developed in an organization.

99% Perspiration
Bryan W. Mattimore
AMACOM, New York, 1994
ISBN: 0-8144-7788-7
A bit like *How to Get Ideas* (listed earlier). Full of lovely examples and stimulating suggestions on how to be creative. Also has good discussion of the role that simple perseverance pays in success.

Innovation
Rosabeth Moss Kanter, John Kao, and Fred Wiersema, editors
Harper Business, New York, 1997
ISBN: 0-8873-0771-X
A collection of challenging and insightful commercial case studies
on how to manage the innovation process. Very good on how to
encourage creativity among staff in unexciting product areas—for
example, Rubbermaid or 3M.

Mind-Sets: Changing the Way You Think

Business Beyond the Box
John O'Keefe
Nicholas Brealy, London 1998
ISBN: 1-8758-8212-1
This is an outstanding book on how the way we think has a signifi-
cant impact on our ability to be successful and on the results we can
achieve in organizations. Very good on how to build up positive
mind-sets as an individual and how to maintain personal motivation.

In Search of America's Best Non-Profits
Richard Steckel and Jennifer Lehman
Jossey-Bass, San Francisco, 1997
ISBN: 0-7879-0445-3
A good book against which to benchmark your nonprofit. Contains
a number of useful and insightful case studies and includes a useful
audit tool. Steckel has also written some other good books on the
idea of entrepreneurship in nonprofits, if you can get hold of them.

Passion at Work
Kevin Thomson
Capstone, Oxford, 1998
ISBN: 1 9000961 61 X
A challenging book on how to be emotionally engaged at work—

and how to involve or engage others through the quality of your communication. Full of models.

Mindmapping and Multiple Intelligences

The Mind Map Book
Tony Buzan and Barry Buzan
BBC Books, London, 1993
ISBN: 0 563 377101 3
The definitive guide to mindmapping and how to use it, by the inventor of the process. Full of great examples and illustrations. Buzan and Buzan link mindmapping strategy to the idea of multiple intelligences.

Head First
Tony Buzan
Thorsons, London, 2000
ISBN: 07 225 404469
A good introduction to multiple intelligences, with useful check-lists and questionnaires to establish your preferences. Lots of ideas on how to use intelligences in your personal life.

Intelligence Reframed: Multiple Intelligences for the Twenty-First Century
Howard Gardner
Perseus Book Group, New York, 2000
ISBN: 0-4650-2611-7
This is the very latest version of Gardner's work, drawing on his two main previous books. It is a useful guide to the use of multiple intelligences in a contemporary setting.

The Mind and the Brain

How the Mind Works
Steven Pinker
W. W. Norton, New York, 1997
ISBN: 0-7139-9130-5
This is an exceptionally well-researched book on the mind and the whole topic of consciousness. Very good for gaining a deeper understanding of the processes through which we deal with experience.

The Right Mind
Robert Ornstein
Harcourt Brace, Orlando, 1997
ISBN: 0-1560-0627-8
A stimulating book on the relationship between the two hemispheres of the brain, written by one of the key figures of the twentieth century on the topic of using the right brain.

Use Both Sides of Your Brain
Tony Buzan
Plume, New York 1990
ISBN: 0-4522-6603-3
One of the earliest popular books on the subject of brain use and different ways to process information. Very good on how memory is developed.

Knowledge and the Learning Organization

The Fifth Discipline
Peter Senge
Currency Doubleday, New York, 1990
ISBN: 0-3852-6095-4
The original book on how to create a learning organization—great examples and ideas on how to develop a learning culture in your organization.

The Fifth Discipline Fieldbook
Peter Senge, Richard Ross, Bryan Smith, Charlotte Roberts, and Art Kleiner
Currency Doubleday, New York, 1994
ISBN: 0-3852-6095-4
A follow-up to the original book on how to develop your learning organization. Full of examples of how the original ideas have been put into practice. Perfect to dip into for inspiration.

References

Chapter One

Obeng, E. *Making Re-Engineering Happen*. London: Pitman, 1994.
Obeng, E. *The Project Leader's Secret Handbook*. London: Pitman, 1996.

Chapter Three

Berners-Lee, T. *Weaving the Web: The Past, Present and Future of the World Wide Web by Its Inventor*. London: Orion, 2001.
Smith, G. *Asking Properly: The Art of Creative Fundraising*. London: The White Lion Press, 1996.
O'Keefe, J. *Business Outside the Box*. London: Nicholas Brealey, 1998.

Chapter Four

Koestler, A. *The Act of Creation*. London: Arkana, 1990, p. 42.

Chapter Five

Gardner, H. *Frames of Mind: The Theory of Multiple Intelligences*. New York: Basic Books, 1983.
Goleman, D. *Emotional Intelligence*. New York: Bantam, 1995.
Gordon, W.J.J., and Poze, T., *The New Art of the Possible*. Cambridge, Mass.: Porpoise Books, 1987, p. 41.
Rosenberg, D. "2000: The Power of Invention." *Newsweek*, Nov. 21, 1997, p. 47.

Chapter Six

Handy, C. *The Age of Unreason*. Boston: Harvard Business School Press, 1990.
Kolb, D. A. *Experiential Learning*. Englewood Cliffs, N. J.: Prentice Hall, 1984, p. 63.

O'Keefe, J. *Business Beyond the Box*. London: Nicholas Brealey, 1998.
Senge, P. *The Fifth Discipline*. New York: Doubleday, 1990.
Senge, P. *The Fifth Discipline Fieldbook*. New York: Doubleday, 1994.

Chapter Seven

Buzan, T. *Use Your Head*. London: BBC Books, 2000.
Buzan, T., and Buzan, B. *The Mind Map Book*. (Rev. ed.) London: BBC Books, 1995.

Chapter Eight

Burnett, K. *Relationship Fundraising*. London: White Lion Press, 1992.
Clegg, B., and Birch, P. *Disorganization: The Handbook of Organizational Strategy*. London: FT/Pitman, 1998.
Coyne, W. "3M." In R. M. Kanter, J. Kao, and F. Wiersema (eds.), *Innovation*. New York: Harper Business, 1997.
Kanter, R. M., Kao, J., and Wiersema, F. (eds.), *Innovation*. New York: Harper Business, 1997.

Chapter Nine

Argyris, C. *Reasoning, Learning and Action: Individual and Organizational Behavior*. San Francisco: Jossey-Bass, 1982.
de Bono, E. *Six Thinking Hats*. New York: Little, Brown, 1999.

Chapter Ten

Fritchie, R. "Managing in the Wild West." *Management Issues*, 1980, 3, 4–10.

Chapter Eleven

Dykson, E. *Job Titles of the Future*. Fast Company, Dec. 1999. At www.fastcompany.com/online/resources/jobtitle.html
Freedman, P. "Lizard Manglers and Other New Jobs." *Sunday Times*, Mar. 19, 2000, p. B12.
Duffy, F. *The New Office*. London: Conran Octopus, 1997, p. 13.

Index